Cryptocurrency:
A Trader's Handbook

A complete guide on how to trade Bitcoin and Altcoins

Marvin Neuefeind

&

Marcin Kacperczyk

Table of Contents

Introduction

With Cryptocurrencies getting more traction day by day, there is a lot of noise around it, varying from scams to millionaires being made on a regular basis. This book offers a broad foundation for everyone who is interested in joining that economic revolution and seeks to know how to start getting a grip on it. This book covers the very basics of technology through challenges of investing in those volatile markets.

We, Marcin Kacperczyk and Marvin Neuefeind, are full-time Cryptocurrency investors, coming from an economic/financial background and developed a great passion for Cryptos. We have seen the best and worst that this market can offer; therefore, we aim to provide an easy introduction to this highly complex and polarising topic. While getting more media and public attention day by day, it is compulsory to teach people how to deal with this revolution.

Why should you read this book?

In this book, we will first show you the underlying theory what Cryptocurrencies are in an easy language, backed by numerous examples. After that, we proceed to the practical part of the book, where we will show you everything you need to know about investments, to minimise your risks and maximise profits. If you are reading this, you might be sceptical or enthusiastic about the possibility to learn more about Cryptocurrencies, either way, we are thankful for your interest in this topic. We want to emphasise, that this book does not require any knowledge in this field and that it is our mission to help people with this complex topic.

To fully prepare you for trading in this volatile market we need to link the theoretical part and the practical applications. It will help you to understand why companies such as Apple, Daimler, Volkswagen, Bosch, Microsoft and many others are working on and with the blockchain technology. In the end, as a result of our trading background, it is vital for us to teach you how to use fundamental and technical analysis so that you can avoid the mistakes we did when we were starting.

Unlike many other books about Cryptocurrencies, which forget about the practical implications and the investing methods, this book is going to provide an easy entrance to the technological side as well as the economic one. At the end of this book, you will be able to analyse coins like stocks based on fundamental analysis and technical analysis. Moreover, you will be able to invest based on the knowledge about industries, growth potential and many others.

Getting Started...

The structure of this book has a specific order, which we recommend maintaining. In the first part we do not only go through basic concepts such as blockchain or mining but also cover security measures. However, if you already understand the technology and want to learn how to invest in Cryptocurrencies solely – feel free to jump straight to the second part of the book. Within the chapters you will find passages in brackets and italic - these sections are examples or more detailed descriptions.

Before we start to answer your questions, we want to emphasise a few points which are very important for us.

1) All of the coins we mention as examples are not meant to be an investment recommendation. This book aims to provide the ability to evaluate coins based on your expertise. None of the cases here is a paid promotion, and they only serve educational purposes.

2) Cryptocurrencies are highly volatile and therefore linked to high risk. This book is not a guide on how to make millions overnight; it provides a sound foundation for underlying technology as well as investment analysis.

3) If you are new to Cryptocurrencies be aware of the people making false recommendations. Because of this, we decided to write this book to help people get a basic understanding of what they are buying, helping them avoid another BitConnect.

Dictionary

In such a modern topic, there are lots of abbreviations and words, which might seem awkward, but in fact are an essential and highly used part of the Cryptoworld. The following abbreviations will help you understand threads, blogs and other sources. You can skip this part and come back to this later, but we would advise you to read through this once before we start.

FOMO - Fear of missing out

(This abbreviation basically describes that a coin is hyped, and investors are eager to buy, willing to pay more than the actual value. They overlook weaknesses or doubts in order not to miss a good opportunity.)

FUD - Fear, Uncertainty, Doubt

(As you probably noticed there are lots of negative articles about Cryptos or Bitcoin in general, FUD describes the outcome of a message. Example: The CEO of JP Morgan said, that Bitcoin is a fraud, therefore he spreads FUD.)

HODL - HOLD

(One of the most used abbreviations in Cryptos is "HODL". It is not a mistake – at least not anymore. Some say it comes from a spelling mistake on a Bitcoin forum, where the topic was "I AM HODLING". Others refer to it as "Hold On for Dear Life". Basically, it describes a type of investor who is holding a certain coin through pumps and dumps.)

ATH - All Time High

(The All Time High describes the highest value a Cryptocurrency reached.)

Shill

("To shill a coin" means that people promote a coin in order to increase the public interest in that coin. Usually YouTube or Twitter "experts" are shilling coins due to their wide range of influence.)

BTFD - Buy the F****** Dip

("Buy The F****** Dip" - When People are selling for no specific reason (maybe FUD), the value will decrease and this would be the perfect time to buy.)

Long - Short

(Long and Short are vocabularies from share trading, usually done with futures and leverage trading. People who position themselves "long", think the price will go up, while people who position themselves "short", think the coin will fall in value.)

ICO - Initial Coin Offering

(This abbreviation is based on the IPO (Initial Public Offering), the standard abbreviation for distributing shares. It means that a Cryptocurrency is launched and the first coins/tokens are sold, before being listed on an exchange.)

Whale

(You will probably someday read, that "whales start buying", or selling. Huge players/investors, who own large stakes of a certain coin are considered as whales.)

Buy wall - Sell wall

(When you take a look at the order book, most exchanges will as well provide a graph for the "market depth". A buy wall is the sum of all the limit orders for buying at the same specific price (green). The sell wall on the other hand is the sum of the selling orders, mostly red.)

Bagholder

(A person holding a high number of coins hoping to make large profits, even through non-profitable times.)

Bear/Bearish - Bullish

(Bear/Bearish means that investors are expecting the stock or coin to fall in value. A bullish movement on the other hand means that investors expect the price to rise.)

Moon

(Or "to the moon", describes that a coin has a strong bullish movement. People who expect a coin to "moon" think that the coin will increase in value. You might have asked yourself, why we selected this cover design and this is the answer to your question. It is an innuendo to the Cryptoworld expecting the Bitcoin to "moon".)

Pump & Dump

(Pump and Dump is a process where investors are investing a lot in a certain coin and then "dump" it, by taking all their money out at one time.)

Green Dildo

(Yes, you read right, a green dildo is a common term in the Crypto-language, meaning massive green candles/price rises.)

FA - TA

(Fundamental Analysis, which describes the evaluation of stock or coin which measures the intrinsic value of an investment. Technical analysis is the analysis based on graphs done with tools.)

Rekt

(Rekt by a coin or getting rekt means that you suffer significant losses.)

Weak Hand

(Having a weak hand means that the investor is selling his/her coins as soon as the price starts to dip, instead of analysing the situation.)

Shitcoin

(A shitcoin is a coin with no intrinsic value. Shitcoins are usually short-term bets to make profits.)

Satoshi - Sat

(Satoshi is not only the first name of Bitcoin founder Satoshi Nakamoto. It is the smallest unit of a Bitcoin, 1 Sat = 0.00000001 BTC.)

Altcoin - Alt season

(An altcoin is every coin except Bitcoin. The alt season is the time of the year in which altcoins are typically increasing their value significantly over the period of few weeks/months.)

Dumb money

(Dumb money describes the process that people tend to invest in a bubble or another rising investment, just because others are doing it.)

Securities and Exchange Commission - SEC

(The US exchange supervisory authority that controls traditional exchanges and their business methods.)

Now, that we are aware of the most common abbreviations and short forms in Cryptocurrencies, we can conclude to the general part of this book.

Part 1

What are Cryptocurrencies?

Blockchain Basics

You might have heard that Cryptos are "unhackable", secure or other characteristics, but let's begin with the fundamental technology.

We will start by taking a look at what kind of blockchains there are and how they work. All types of Cryptocurrencies are based on a distribution system; therefore, they are often described as distributed ledgers. Here the information is not saved in a single place, but on millions of computers in the network. Each computer saves either the full or only parts of the blockchain.

The most used form is the public blockchain, where everyone has access and can read and add information. Due to this freedom, this type of blockchain is usually the slowest version. Users are participating anonymously/pseudo-anonymously.

(The latter means that the user is anonymously active, but transactions could be calculated backwards to the end user; therefore, they are not 100% anonymous.)

The second possible type is a consortium blockchain, which only uses specific crossover points for validation. As a result of this only participants of the "consortium" have access to the blockchain, this guarantees a faster process, and the creators can decide if participants are public or anonymous. This form will be very interesting for business adaptions, which we will discuss and explain at a later point of this book in greater detail.

The third type is an entirely private blockchain; here transactions are validated by a certain amount of validators. The creator can decide who can add information or see it. This results in a very fast processing time, and the creator usually knows each validator.

You may question yourself, what is a blockchain or how can I imagine it. As the name suggests, the blockchain is a linkage of several blocks. The speciality is that each block is generating code, based on the content it carries, which is saved in the consecutive block with other new information. But let's look at an example, which might be easier to understand:

(Assuming "Peter lends Helen 50€". The Block in the blockchain is saving this information and produces a code based on the order of the letters and numbers used – let's say AAAAA. If Helen would get access to one block and changes the information to "Helen lends Peter 50€" the outcome of this block would not be AAAAA, but BBBBB. Therefore, the blockchain would directly show that some information has been changed, because of the error report of other computers in the decentralised network.)

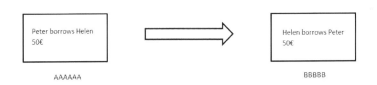

Blockchain as a basis for a Currency

The History of the blockchain is strongly connected to the history of Bitcoin; therefore, a lot of people confuse those two and might even take it for the same. In 2008, Satoshi Nakamoto published the White Paper "Bitcoin: A Peer to

Peer electronic cash system", which is the foundation for Cryptocurrencies today.

Most Cryptocurrencies are based on the blockchain technology. This technology is based on four main characteristics.

Firstly, the decentralisation, meaning that the data is not saved on a single computer/server in an only place. On the contrary, most blockchains are saved on millions of computers simultaneously.

Because of that, the blockchain cannot be changed. Once a transaction is confirmed on the blockchain it is nearly impossible to change the saved information. *(To change it, all nodes where the blockchain is kept, would have to be replaced simultaneously.)*

The underlying principle is called consensus, meaning that the community has to agree on what happens and what does not happen. One way to reach this consensus is called "mining". It is part of the proof of work system, which we will discuss in the next chapter.

Another critical point is transparency. In almost every Cryptocurrency, transactions can be tracked, and users can see who added blocks in a "proof-of-work" system.

In some cases, there also is a "Rich-List" stating the addresses with the highest amount of coins.

(This can be helpful to see how well the coins are distributed. This does not mean that people can see the name of someone! The only visible information is the public address.)

Lastly and probably one of the biggest threats to the old financial system - the transfer of values. While banks take one business day or even longer, depending on the size of the transaction and the destination, values can be shifted a lot faster with Cryptocurrencies. (10-30min, or even instant transactions are not rare anymore.)

Regarding this, the transaction fees can be 0, so that means the consumer does not need an intermediary. (Those points will be discussed at a later stage in more detail.)

Before reaching the functional part of blockchains, we will have a quick view on how the blockchain recognises accounts and how they are used.

How do I access the blockchain?

All of you will probably have a bank account or any other kind of account whether it is used for mailing, gaming or any other purpose. Those accounts are all saved in one place, which allocates the account name to the account user. In a decentralised network, this is not how it works, due to the reason that there is no central instance controlling and maintaining the accounts.

In a decentralised network such as Bitcoin, users differentiate between private keys and public addresses. You might already assume what each one could be.

When you are creating an email account, you will first check whether the wanted address is already taken and then you choose a password. By creating blockchain access, this is working the other way around. The private key is a randomly created code which is your password and allocation of resources at once. It usually contains 32 or 64 characters and numbers. It might look like this:

48DHQUS5CBG8RHTMS268F5S4DGANBGD53HTU ETDG654G2F158D2F3G4CBVMD4F5G

After the private key was created - this can be done by yourself using random characters or by a wallet - the public address will appear automatically based on the private key.

(In case you are wondering whether it is easy to guess your private address by knowing the public address - it is not.

The mathematics behind it is very complicated and based on several cryptographic formulas such as SHA256.

The important thing to know it is quite easy (for a computer) to calculate the public address based on your private address, but it cannot be done the opposite way. Computers would need to "guess" the right combination which would take millions of years.)

The public address will then be your "account name", meaning if someone wants to send you money he will need the public address. **Never give away your private key!**

A blockchain and a private key CANNOT be hacked, the only thing that could be hacked is your computer where the private key is saved. We will have a better look at wallets at a later stage of this book.

The most important thing for you to remember is: the private key is your password and allocation of resources on the blockchain. If you give it to someone, this someone can control your assets. If you lose it, your coins are gone. The public address, on the other hand, is like your account number at your bank - you can share it without any doubt to receive assets.

In case you want to track your transaction within the blockchain and see how many validations it has already received, you can easily access with the so-called "block explorer". Here you can see the latest blocks which were mined and the transactions which were contained. If you are looking for your transaction, you can either get redirected from the exchange (if you used one) or search for the address or transaction on this site (https://blockexplorer.com/).

The difference between a token and a coin

By looking up different currencies, you will undoubtedly recognise that some are called coins (which is the most common way), and some are called tokens. A Cryptocurrency can be either the one or the other. Firstly, as you might know already a Cryptocurrency is called Cryptocurrency, because it requires solving cryptographic tasks to validate information.

"Coins" are the most represented kind of Cryptocurrencies. In general, a coin has its very own underlying technology, the blockchain. That means every currency which is not built on top of another blockchain and uses its source code is defined as a coin. For example Bitcoin, Litecoin, Dogecoin and so on.

(In theory, a token is not an altcoin, but is generally declared as such.)

"Tokens" on the other hand are built on top of another Cryptocurrency, such as Ethereum or NEO. Tokens are used to compensate the underlying technology for their services, such as the mining power to approve transactions or the system as a whole. Therefore, tokens are often called "fuel" for platforms. Ethereum, for example, has erc20 tokens, which are the "fuel" of the Ethereum blockchain.

(In case you want to see all of the coins and tokens you can go to www.CoinMarketCap.com, which is the place you can check all the coin values, and filter between "all", "coins" and "tokens".)

What does scalability mean?

Scalability is an often-mentioned issue of Bitcoin and other Cryptocurrencies. It describes the ability of a network or system to process an increasing demand for data. In financial markets, scalability points out how well a financial institution is capable of handling a growing demand. Regarding companies, people refer to scalability as the potential for increasing profits and revenues.

In the Cryptoworld this usually refers to the issue whether the coin is capable of being used as everyday currency. That means if a Cryptocurrency has no problem with an increasing number of transactions or even becomes better, it can be considered scalable. On the other hand, if a Cryptocurrency slows down with higher demand, it is not scalable and therefore has a scalability problem.

(Bitcoin has this scalability problem and is trying to solve it with "lighting network", which we will discuss at a later stage. Most currencies which are based on a Proof of Work system appear to have scalability issues.)

Now you have a broad idea what the blockchain technology is, but how do the validations work? In the next paragraph, we will take a look at how it works, meaning the differentiation between "proof of work", "proof of stake" and others.

How does the blockchain work?

As we know already, the blockchain is based on several blocks which are connected to each other, containing different information. To add a block to the chain, the validator needs to fulfil specific tasks, depending on the algorithm which is used within the blockchain. In this chapter, we will take a look at how each block is validated and what different ways there are of running a blockchain.

Nodes and Masternodes

In the previous chapter, we talked about how the blockchain is constructed and that the community needs to create a consensus to add information. Validators which create new blocks approve this information.

When we are looking at this in greater detail, we have to differentiate between nodes and miners. Nodes can be divided into full and light nodes; the latter is a user. That means he is saving only parts of the blockchain on his computer and his primary interest is to send and receive payments. Those payments are rewarded by the user with a transaction fee/mining fee.

(In theory, it is possible not to pay any transaction fees, but miners prefer transactions with fees. Therefore, it can take years for your transaction to be processed, if you decided not to offer a reward/fee or a lower one than standard.)

Full nodes, on the other hand, are saving the complete blockchain and forward transaction/information to create a consensus.

By looking at coin comparisons, you may find that coins such as DASH have masternodes and others such as Bitcoin do not. Masternodes are another feature the blockchain can offer. In this paragraph, we will explain what these are and why some coins have it, and others have not.

The Cryptocurrency called DASH established masternodes. They are servers, which offer a service that regular miners or nodes cannot process. Before a masternode can be used, the user needs to put in a stake to be able to create one. *(In the DASH -network this would be 1000 DASH, currently around 500,000$ (March 2018)).*

The tasks of a masternode can vary within different currencies, but usually, they are able to process instant or anonymous transactions. Furthermore, they protect the network from attacks and have a higher voting right, when it comes to decisions regarding the blockchain. These characteristics are perfect for running smart contracts.

Of course, staking that much money will be rewarded differently than usual mining. Even though it depends on the Cryptocurrency, a masternode can earn 5-20% of a given block reward.

Forks

A Fork in the Cryptoworld has nothing to do with food or agriculture. Concerning blockchains, a fork is a moment where the blockchain splits into two (or more) different ways.

We know already that one block follows another, but sometimes the blockchain splits, which can have various reasons. No matter what was the cause of it, the history of the blockchain always remains the same. Reasons for the split can be either small or large, for example, an update or a significant change which divides the community. An example of such a small change can be a "soft-fork" (this means that blockchain is getting updated). Usually, the old version still works; therefore, the user does not have to follow the soft-fork.

(A major exception was the Bitcoin's soft-fork at the end of July 2017, here the Segwit update did not allow the old version to be used; hence many people did not want to follow and decided to initiate a "hard-fork".)

A hard-fork is the opposite of the soft-fork - here the blockchain splits after a certain block, and a new coin is created. The paths of the two coins are irrevocably separated.

(Continuing with the Bitcoin example: The issue was there were two sides of users and miners. The first side aimed to keep the block size small, to only use the blockchain for big transactions. The smaller ones would be done with the lighting network (will be explained later). This group of people is currently using Bitcoin. The other group wanted to increase the block size because for them all transactions should be saved on the blockchain. This group is currently using "Bitcoin Cash / Bcash".)

You might ask yourself what consequences this has on the holder of this coin. When such fork is initiated, and the blockchain splits, the basis for both currencies (the old and the new one) has the same blockchain history. Therefore, if someone was holding for example Bitcoin at the end of July 2017, his stake was recognised before the fork. Consequently, he has the same amount of those coins on both blockchains.

(If you had 10 BTC before the fork, after the fork you had 10 BTC and 10 BCH (Bitcoin Cash).)

But - and this is a vital part most people forget about - in order to claim the coins, you have to be in possession of your private key! Only with the private key, it is possible to control the coins on both chains. Only in sporadic cases, exchanges offer the service of claiming the coins for you and distributing the new currency.

A fork is a highly sensitive topic for a Cryptocurrency and therefore most of the times hard to judge. We will come back to this topic at a later stage of this book when we are talking about best investment strategies for such events.

The next pages will deal with the general algorithms a blockchain can use. *(It does sound more complicated than it is.)*

The Blockchain

Proof of Work (PoW)

Proof of Work is probably the best-known basis of the blockchain. You might have heard of "mining" and several critics stating that the energy consumption is extremely high, but let's have a look at it to see what this means.

We have already learned each block of the blockchain needs to be validated to create a consensus. The proof of work method means that a "miner" is solving cryptographic tasks and receive a reward for solving it. *(That is where the name Cryptocurrency comes from.)*

These tasks are complex calculations which are addressed by testing different solutions. With solving the calculation, the miner approves that the transaction which was saved on the block was made accurately. Usually, the difficulty of the tasks increases continuously. The rewards per block differ strongly from Cryptocurrency to Cryptocurrency.

(In 2009 as Bitcoin started each miner got 50 BTC per block. But every 210,000 coins the rewards halves. This happens approximately every four years. Currently (2018) each miner receives 12.5 BTC per block.)

You might ask, what will happen if all coins of a Cryptocurrency are mined? Miners can also be rewarded with fees, which might increase if the rewards of mining in BTC go down. Mining is the only way new coins can get released into a network.

Most of the well-known Cryptocurrencies are using the proof of work algorithms, such as Bitcoin, Litecoin, Zcash, Siacoin and others.

Still, this method is heavily criticised, because solving the tasks to validate a block is not only time-consuming but also consumes a lot of energy, which makes them very expensive.

This is one of the reasons why most of the best graphics cards by ASUS or NVIDIA are sold out because miners need them.

(Please note, when we talk about miners who "solve" tasks, they do not calculate 2+2=X. They "solve" complex tasks by trying out different values.)

The often-criticised environmental problem is hard to judge - right now experts estimate a total electricity consumption (for 2017) of Bitcoin-mining of 17 terawatt hours, which conforms about 0.1% of the global electricity consumption. On the first sight this looks like a lot for a currency which is not used by many people, but if we compare it to gold, for example, we can see that this is not as high as it first seemed. To make it easier, we can compare the total production of Bitcoin to the total output of gold and see how many barrels of oil they have consumed. Bitcoin (translated electricity to oil) consumes 6.6 million barrels per year (2017 estimation), while it took 123.2 million barrels to produce all the gold of 2017.

Right now, mining of the prominent Cryptocurrencies is not profitable anymore for most private people, due to the rising difficulty and high electricity costs (it still can be, when you decide to mine small market cap coins). That is also why there are so many "mining farms" in Iceland or anywhere else where electricity is cheap. Private people can now rent a graphics card there to mine for example BTC.

As a result, lately, the risk of a 51-percent-attack rose. A 51-percent-attack is the possibility of a mining pool manipulating the transactions due to their dominant position. This means that a mining pool with 51% of the mining power could double spend the underlying Cryptocurrency ("selfish mining"). In game theory, there is a scenario called "Tragedy of the Commons", which is stating that a good is produced in lower quantities than the public desires, or consumed in greater quantities than desired.

Related to Bitcoin, this means there might be a point where the general incentives for mining will drop (when all Bitcoins are mined and fill only reward miners). This results in the increased possibility of 51-percent-attacks as the difficulty will fall as well.

(Double spending describes a process in which one person can distribute his/her assets twice. Imagine Person A owns 10€. If he has 51% of the mining power, he can send the 10€ to Person A and receive the consideration. After that, he would be able to continue a new block path and spend the 10€ again.)

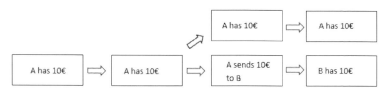

Lightning Network

After getting a closer look at the system of Proof of Work (PoW) you will probably see that this system is very likely to have a significant scalability issue - this is correct. Bitcoin is fighting against this problem and has found an interesting approach to solve it. The solution is called "lightning network" and describes a method of processing transactions off-chain. *(For comparison: While Visa can approve up to 4,000 transactions per second, Bitcoin can process seven without the lightning network.)*

This type of process promises to reduce the high transaction fees to a minimum and increase the scalability to a maximum of up to billions per second. It sounds too good to be true, but let's take a look at how they are planning to achieve it.

The lightning network can be broadly described as a peer to peer application which is added to the existing Bitcoin blockchain. This system is called "payment channels" and enables the possibility of transactions working without passing the blockchain. One payment channel is a connection between two users, who can send BTC to one another. These small transactions are only saved on the blockchain if both users sign at the end and close this channel. The users can determine the duration of it. This enables the chance that not every transaction needs to be saved on the blockchain, but only the outcome of several transactions. This means that it requires only two operations - one to open the channel and one to close it.

(You can visualise it the following way: Let's say there is Paul who is buying a coffee every morning before work. If he wants to purchase the coffee without the lightning network, his transaction would need to be validated and saved on the blockchain. This could cost more than the coffee itself, and the transaction could take up to hours to be transmitted.

The lightning network can be imagined as a safe which contains a balance sheet. Paul and the coffee shop create a payment channel, and Paul is contributing 100€, while the coffee shop is contributing nothing because it expects payments. The first transaction needs to be done, and both of their contributions are saved on a balance sheet.

This balance sheet is saved on the blockchain and is visible to everyone and secure. Whenever Paul wants to buy a coffee at this shop, he can go there and make his payment. The payment will be made by changing the balance sheet. Let's assume a coffee costs 3€. The balance sheet is changed from: "Paul 100€ and Shop 0€" to "Paul 97€ and Shop 3€".

Each party gets a copy of the changed balance, and Paul receives a coffee. This could go on forever because Paul is able to fund as much as he wants. Both parties can close the channel at any time they want; they only need to provide the latest balance sheet, which will be saved on the blockchain.)

Furthermore, the network is creating indirect connections as well. Meaning, that a transaction from A to D can be processed if A has a payment channel with C and C has one with D. There is no necessity in creating an extra one between A and D.

(Back to our example: If Laura wants to buy a coffee at that shop and does not have a payment channel with that shop, but with Paul, then she can use Paul as an intermediary.)

One downside is this system requires the intermediary to have enough money in the appropriate payment channel. There is another issue from a financial point of view. The capital which is in the payment channel is fixed and therefore cannot be used for investments or others. One solution could be that a company is taking place as an intermediary, but that has not been the case.

Fact is, the lightning network can be the saviour of Bitcoin's image not being suitable as an everyday currency, but there is still a lot of work to do.

(The picture below visualises the explained.)

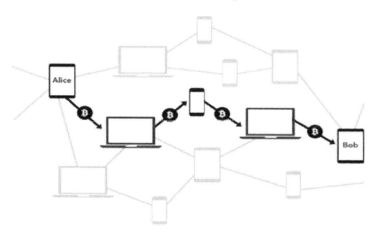

(The picture was taken from: http://coinews.io/en/category/1-kripto/article/81-francuzskaya-kompaniya-uspeshno-protestirovala-lightning-network)

Atomic Swaps

The foundation of atomic swaps is the lightning network. Without that system running, it is not possible to initiate the process. Atomic swaps are far less complicated than they sound. It describes a procedure of trading Cryptocurrencies without a central party – an exchange.

(For example, Paul owns 1 BTC and wants to buy LTC. Laura, on the other hand, holds 10 LTC and intends to buy BTC. Without the system of atomic swaps, both parties would have to go to an exchange and place an order for selling or buying. Now, with atomic swaps, both parties can agree on a price/ratio and trade the possessions immediately. Let's say 1 BTC is worth 10 LTC. Then Paul sends his BTC to the Bitcoin blockchain and Laura sends her LTC to the Litecoin blockchain. Both transactions will then be linked and can be claimed by a secret number.)

(In theory, this could even go so far, that if there were different lightning networks on different blockchains, the user could create a cross-channel payment channel and trade coins from one currency to another immediately.)

The whole process is far less complicated than it might appear to be and it has a chance to become a real game changer and a huge benefit of Bitcoin's blockchain. All Cryptocurrencies which are based on the Bitcoin blockchain can use atomic swaps.

Due to the high speed of progress, it is hard to predict whether the lightning network and all of its features will be the final solution. It could be that they come up with a better alternative in the near future since the lightning network still is in a development stage.

Proof of Stake (PoS)

Proof of Stake is one the most significant alternatives to the proof of work system, which we studied in the paragraph above. Unlike actively mining a Cryptocurrency to create a consensus, users of the proof of stake algorithm are not proactively "working" for their rewards, as they are rewarded for "staking". This method can be compared to interest payments by banks.

In greater detail, this means, a user of (let's take NEO, which is one of the most famous PoS coins) is rewarded for holding NEOs in his wallet. The miner, as well as the "staker", seeks to find a specific value to solve an equation in order to validate a transaction/block. But unlike PoW, where the rewards depend on the processing power, in PoS the rewards depend on the number of coins someone is holding.

In the Proof of Stake algorithm, the staker is guessing values to solve the equation, while the width of the possible guesses again depends on the stake someone has in his wallet. The rewards for created blocks and the transaction fees are distributed depending on the percentage of the total stake and the duration the coins were held.

(Concluding that - you can earn about 5.5% p.a. in NEO for example.)

The most significant advantages of this algorithm are that it consumes a lot less energy than PoW and it does not have the risk of centralisation, as it might be possible with a 51%-attack.

But this method does have a downside as well. A lot of people are stating, that this method favours the rich, which is only partly right. The critics are right about the consensus power, meaning the more coins you have, the more "staking-power" you have. But the risk of using this to manipulate the blockchain is minimal because coins can neither be created out of thin air nor can be faked. In addition to that, the general incentives for participating in such criminal activity are comparably low, because staking has no costs and staker would "destroy" the whole currency.

Another theoretical problem is the "Nothing-at-Stake" issue. In theory, this means that users might be able to double-spend their money. *(This process is quite complicated and is not vital for further understanding).*

This problem assumes the following - there are two blocks created simultaneously, which are both valid. Now, in a PoW system, people would decide whether going with the one or the other because they are consuming resources for mining.

In PoS 90% can go way A and 90% can go way B because it is all about maximising the fees. Now it could be the case, that a party makes a transaction on way B and then after it gets confirmed, supports way A to double spend the money. This is possible because you are not risking any resources, as PoS does not burn money, time or energy.

(For those of you who have not understood it and wanted to, this video is visualising it quite well https://www.youtube.com/watch?v=pzIl3vmEytY).

As mentioned above this is a highly theoretical problem which in our opinion will never occur.

Delegated Proof of Stake

The delegated Proof of Stake algorithm is a newer and more democratic version of the original Proof of Stake algorithm.

(The most famous representative of this coin is probably STEEM.)

Just like in a democratic system a stakeholder is passing on his voting rights to a delegate or witness (representative). This delegate is acting on behalf of his elector and confirms blocks. This system supports decentralisation as well as democracy.

Trustless Proof of Stake (TPoS)

Another exciting technology which still is an insider tip, as there is only one coin using this technology, is called "Trustless Proof of Stake" (TPoS). The TPoS was invented by XSN (formerly known as POSW) and describes a system where users of the network can stake their coins without running any device. The clue behind it is that users have the possibility of selecting a merchant who is staking the coins for you, in return for a share of your stake.

The main advantage is that you do not need to be the one staking the coins. This is done by a TPoS contract, where the user gives the merchant the right to stake coins – this contract can be cancelled at any time.

In the end, this is an exciting alternative to many other staking coins, as you need no staking equipment nor lose the control over your assets. By diversifying your portfolio, this could be an interesting factor as there will be a possibility of holding the coins on a Ledger (we will come back to this at a later stage).

Proof of Burn (PoB)

Another alternative system is Proof of Burn, which like PoS, is an energy saving method. Here, the miner sends coins to an unused address and receives points in reward. These points are comparable to the hash-rate of mining and are therefore used to validate blocks and transactions.

It is crucial that this algorithm is only working in connection with other mining possibilities - to be able to burn coins, they have to be created in the first place.

The idea behind it is that an attack would be very difficult and carries an enormous element of risk, unlike the PoS system where we already looked at the "Nothing-at-Stake" issue.

Proof of Importance (PoI)

The system proof of importance, which is used by NEM (one of the largest currencies out there), is not only rare but also has enormous potential.

In this algorithm, the user is collecting points on an importance score. This score can be an indicator how trustworthy the member is. The users are validating transactions, just like in every other blockchain algorithm with the exception that everyone, regardless of his/her wealth, starts at 0.

If a person is making false approvals or tries to betray the system, their rating is lowered. Therefore, their possibility to receive rewards and add transactions is decreasing. You can compare it to financial advisors - you trust the one with good ratings and maybe personal recommendations, but if they are rated negatively you will probably stay away.

NEM is requesting 10,000 coins to be able to get such score, which is about 4000$. *(This can be adapted, when the currency becomes more popular. If you are interested in the coin, you can read further details of the scoring system in their White Paper.)*

A theoretical problem would occur, if there were no control by the currency itself, such as NEM, and people would be able to rate each other. A criminal organisation might be able to upvote themselves. But there are many ways to protect oneself against it, and therefore this is not a serious issue.

Proof of Signature (PoSign)

Currently, the only Cryptocurrency which uses Proof of Signature is Xtrabytes (XBY). This technology carries an interesting approach, which aims to be the best out of both worlds, PoS and PoW.

Xtrabytes uses a network which is run by real nodes and virtual network nodes. The latter are smaller nodes which are based on physical nodes. The transactions are validated by the nodes online and are double checked by the nodes which are offline by the time the transaction is transmitted. In addition to that, the network employs a system called PULSE (Ping Unified Leger Synchronization Equalizer).

PULSE alerts and selects the nodes when a transaction is transmitted, these transactions will be ordered by time and then be processed. This system enables the possibility of approving up to 10,000 transactions per second.

A fundamental characteristic of this method is the lack of block mining that means, this algorithm is not in danger of a 51-percent-attack.

This technology is an exciting opportunity for the future due to its lack of energy waste and high scalability.

There are many other algorithms, but we will stop at this point because, concerning the blockchain, the ones we mentioned are the most important ones.

The blockchain is not the only basis for Cryptocurrencies. On the contrary, there are two other foundations of Cryptocurrencies: Tangle and Hashgraph.

Tangle

Tangle is a strong alternative to the blockchain technology, which aims to reduce costs and enhance the transaction time to be scalable enough for "Internet of Things". The background of this technology is to serve economic mechanisms, such as autonomous payments of machines and internet of things.

(For those who have never heard of the Internet of things, it describes how computers are making payments independently from the human being owning it. This can be extended to computers communicating amongst themselves. This may sound like science, but in fact, this is a very current topic.)

The Tangle has significant potential, but it remains to be seen whether it will succeed or not. Either way, we will explain the specialities of this technology in the following paragraph. Also, we will come back to this topic at a later stage of this book, when we are talking about prospects and adaption possibilities.

(The most famous Cryptocurrency which is based on the Tangle network is called IOTA, which is one of the ten most valuable coins (March 2018).)

What is Tangle?

First of all, Tangle, as well as the classic blockchain, is a distributed network, meaning there is no central instance controlling the currency. Transactions need to create a consensus in order to be validated. You might remember how the blockchain looked like – it was one block following the other in a specific order. Tangle, on the other hand, is entirely different. Here, the organisation of the blocks is not in order. On the contrary, it is confused within itself as you can see next:

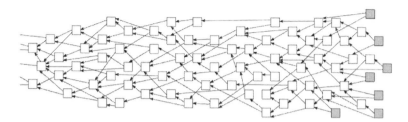

(The picture was taken from: https://www.nasdaq.com/article/what-is-the-tangle-and-is-it-blockchains-next-evolutionary-step-cm911074)

The system is working from left to right. Here, the grey blocks (tips) are the most current endings of the blockchain. You will hopefully remember that in the blockchain technology we had different possibilities of mining new blocks in order to create a consensus.

(Revision: The Proof of Work algorithm uses miners to validate transactions. These miners are rewarded by the transaction fees and the mined coins.)

If someone wants to make a transaction within the Tangle network, this is not necessary. To be able to submit a transaction, you need to approve two other transactions which need to be validated. Some blocks may be confirmed more than one time, as it is based on a random selection. This means that we do not have the distinction between a node, full node and miner. Every node becomes a miner if he wants to make a transaction.

Based on this, it allows the user to make 0-transaction-fee transactions. Another benefit is in contrast to the classic blockchain algorithm - the more people are using a Cryptocurrency like IOTA (Tangle based), the faster the transaction will be transmitted. In short: Tangle has unlimited scalability.

Contrary to the classic Blockchain, Tangle is described as quantum-safe, which means that the significant threat of becoming hackable when quantum computers will be invented does not exist.

Regarding the Tangle network IOTA is using, the network is working on a regional basis. That means that people around you will approve transactions.

(For example: When you are in the western part of Germany, you need to approve prevalent transactions from the Western Germany. Same goes on with every regional location.)

What are the issues of Tangle?

A problem in this system is that the primary incentive for every transaction is to approve its predecessor – whether it is right or wrong. Of course, the wrong transaction will be found and cancelled, but if a transaction has a false predecessor, it risks not becoming validated. As this technology is entirely new, it is not proven yet, whether it works accurately or not.

Another theoretical problem is the vulnerability to 34-percent-attacks. In theory, the Tangle can be insecure if a single party is controlling 34% or more of the network. The most popular currency IOTA is solving that issue with a node called "coordinator".

(This is a more powerful node, which is controlling the network. The coordinator is collecting "snapshots" of the Tangle and is saving them to secure the network.)

This node, on the other hand, is saving the data centralised and therefore against the "morals" of Cryptocurrencies. Even though IOTA explained that it is only a temporary move to protect the network it has raised some critic's voices.

Conclusion

The Tangle technology is far different from what we have known and is an interesting alternative to the blockchain. Because it is entirely new, there still are a few points which might cause problems. At this point, we are not able to judge, whether this technology will succeed or be a good investment, but due to its high adaptability possibilities, it is highly fascinating. We will come back to this methodology at a later stage of this book when we are talking about practical implications.

Hashgraph

The last consensus method we will discuss in this book is called Hashgraph. This technology is the youngest model of creating a consensus without the blockchain. It made a lot of noise at the end of 2017 and has a massive potential for the future; therefore, we will take a closer look at it to see what the whole thing is about.

What is Hashgraph?

As we already mentioned this is another alternative to the blockchain, and for some people, this is the next level of distributed ledgers (decentralised networks). This technology is aiming to be a voting algorithm.

(A voting algorithm is a way to validate transactions on a peer to peer basis. That means the nodes are "talking" to each other and approve a transaction after reaching a consensus:

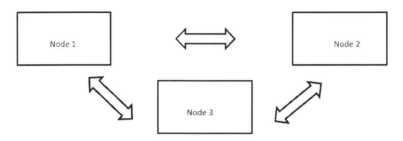

(This way of approving the transaction is excellent because it is not possible to centralise it. It is also very elaborate because a lot of messages would have to be sent. Therefore, this method was not used until Hashgraph came up.)

The idea Hashgraph invented to make it work is called "gossip protocol". As the name might reveal, this protocol is based on one node giving some information to another node. This node is chosen randomly and then tells everything he knows the next one and so on. As you might know from real life, gossips can spread very fast, and this is precisely what the gossip protocol is aiming to do. The information that is spread across the nodes does contain three main questions: 1) What? → What happened? (transaction wise) 2) Who? → Who provided the information? 3) When? → When was that information provided?

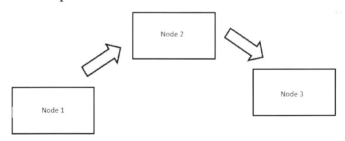

This is the reason why Hashgraph is claimed to be very fair. *(Fairness is related to the order the transactions are processed. You might remember that in PoW, the miner picks a transaction from the one willing to pay the highest transaction fee. This is what is meant by fairness).* Hashgraph promises that the transactions are processed in the order they are submitted. *(Ordered by the third question, the WHEN?)*

The way the voting approach is working here is called "virtual voting". It is not necessary that every node is talking to each node, simply because the last node "knows" everything his predecessors did know. This procedure makes it a lot easier for the system to work faster and more efficient.

(Hashgraph claims to be able to process 250,000 transactions per second.)

What are the issues of Hashgraph?

Unfortunately, this technology has a significant disadvantage. The technology is patented, meaning you cannot use it without the permission of the patent holding instance. To use it you have to request a software kit, but it is not open source. That means that currently it cannot be used as a basis for a Cryptocurrency.

What the company behind Hashgraph (Swirlds) is going to do with the technology remains to be seen. Many people assume that they want to keep this technology for the industry to serve large corporations.

Conclusion

Fact is that this technology is very interesting and has a vast potential. Therefore, it is essential for us to teach you the main characteristics, in case it will succeed someday. Depending on the patent right, it could be the case that this technology might be relevant for the Cryptoworld in the near future.

Wallets & security

One of the most important topics about Cryptocurrencies is one of the less researched. There are many ways to store and secure Cryptocurrencies, and we will take a look at each possibility and its advantages or disadvantages. You have to keep in mind that a Cryptocurrency is a purely digital asset; therefore, the one controlling your private key has unlimited access to your assets. It is crucial for us to emphasise the importance of this topic. Similar to your bank account the main rule is, protect your PIN / private key and only share it with the ones you can trust 100%.

What is a Wallet?

A wallet can be imagined as a way to save your private keys. You will probably remember that you access your assets with a private key which is connected to your stake of coins in the network. There are different ways of securing that private key, and that is what we call a wallet. The user has several means of securing its private key, such as "paper wallet", "soft wallet", "hard wallet", "mind wallets", "exchanges" and the difference between "hot wallets" and "cold wallets".

Cold Wallets

The so-called "cold wallet" is every type of wallet where the private key is stored offline, with no connection to the internet.

Paper Wallet

A paper wallet is probably the most secure way to store coins but at the same time the most inconvenient. A paper wallet is nothing else than creating a private key and writing it down on a piece of paper.

(There are a couple of fundamental things for you to take care of when storing coins like this:

1) *Generate the private key by yourself and do NOT use an online generator.*

2) *Write the private key with your hand in clear patterns, with water and heat proof pencil. Remember this key might have to "survive" years or decades.*

3) *Do NOT print it out, your printer or computer might save it.*

4) *Make more than one copy and distribute them at different places. In case of a robbery, natural catastrophe or others.*

5) *Do NOT save the key on any electronic device.)*

If you follow these rules, your private cannot be stolen easily. This type of storage is very safe, but unfortunately very inconvenient because you cannot access your wallet quickly. Theoretically, you have to change the private seed every time you are entering the private key, in case of spy software. In which degree this is relevant for you, lays within your responsibility. You can save the public address on your computer without any doubt, as we learned already, knowing the public address does not reveal your private key.

Brain Wallet

A brain wallet means you remember the private key and therefore do not need any copy of it. To be honest, it is doubtful that regular people can remember a private key, because usually, they are quite long. The risk of forgetting your private key is very high, and then there is no way of recovering it.

Hot Wallets

These are the wallets which are saved on a device with internet connection. Hot wallets do not have to be insecure, but it is essential to understand their risks because today you need to expect that everything can be hacked.

Soft Wallet

Soft wallets are a very popular way of saving the private keys. They describe software which serves as a safe for your private key, where you need to come up with a password to protect it. It is important to know that theoretically your computer can be hacked; therefore, the password of the soft wallet should not be saved anywhere on the computer as well.

(For your safety, we advise you to write down your private key on an extra paper, just like a paper wallet.)

In case your device is broken, you can easily access your coins if you made a backup of your private key. If not, your coins are lost. Therefore, it is vital to ALWAYS have a backup plan -think about the "What if".

Hard Wallet

A hard wallet is a combination of a cold wallet and a hot wallet. This type of wallet was created by companies such as Ledger or Trezor, which created a wallet that can be compared to an USB-Stick. Even if it looks similar, it is not an ordinary one, as you need to enter a PIN code to access the wallet and all of the private keys on it.

The company Ledger, for example, does have a backup of every data saved on your wallet; therefore, it is possible to restore it even if it was destroyed. *(It does have pros and cons, at this point we do not want to say whether it is good or bad that they create backups).*

The speciality of Trezor is that you are required to touch the device AND enter the PIN to enter your assets.

Other manufacturers of hard wallets do not offer this service, but it is essential to know that Ledger has this characteristic. Besides, even here it is important to create a paper wallet as a backup in case you lose your data.

Exchanges

Exchanges are the most popular way of storing coins because it is the most convenient way. If you store your coins on an exchange, you can easily trade them and send them anywhere you want. This is due to the reason that the exchange administers your private keys for you.

However, this method of storing coins is highly risky. Remember you are not directly in possession of the private key which means, that if the exchange is hacked, you can lose your coins. This is the main reason why many people think a blockchain can be hacked or hackers can easily steal your coins. It is true that in 2017 a couple of exchanges were hacked and a lot of money has been stolen, but this was not because Cryptocurrencies are hard to store. This was due to the reason that many people did not care about storing possibilities.

Deterministic Wallets

When you are using a hot wallet, your public address may change from time to time. You might have recognised that some exchanges enable the possibility to generate a new address (or you were afraid that your coins are lost because you sent them to the wrong address). First of all, this mechanism is nothing to be scared of!

(This technology is called "deterministic wallets" and is a feature which aims to improve security. Let's take the IOTA light Wallet as an example. The first thing you do is to choose a "seed" which contains (in IOTAs case) 24 words. These words can be chosen randomly and are now the seed

of your private keys. Based on that the wallet creates a first private key and a public address, where you can receive coins. The next time you enter your wallet, you can recreate a public address, or it changes automatically. The reason is that based on your first private key and in connection to your seed the wallet calculates a new private key where you can receive coins now. To access all of the private keys which were generated, your wallet calculates the following keys and sums up the total of your balance.)

This procedure provides a higher security standard because your coins are now split. It is, as we already learnt, impossible to "hack" a private key, but in case someone guesses it right or steals the original one from a digital copy, he cannot steal the total amount of money. Even if a private key is given out twice (that could theoretically happen, but it is more likely to win the lottery five times in a row and then die by the hit of a bolt of lightning) you would only lose a part of your money.

How should I secure my assets?

There are a couple of important rules to follow, and it is essential for you to think about the best way to store your assets.

First, it is crucial that you choose your wallet depending on your requirements. That means, if you are into day trading you have different demands than someone who is willing to hold the assets for years. Be aware of the risks that come with exchange possessing your private keys.

Moreover, be aware that some shitcoins can have wallets which contain viruses. Therefore, it is essential that you research the Cryptocurrency and evaluate if it is trustworthy or not. You should avoid downloading any programs or contents with an uncertain background!

It cannot be repeated often enough - you need to have a backup plan. Store your access to your wallets, exchanges or ledgers in different geographical places and secure them against robbery, natural catastrophes and so on.

Generally, there is no best way to store Crypto assets. In the following paragraph, we will discuss some safety measures. Whether you follow them and to which extent lays within your responsibility.

VPN

A VPN is a Virtual Private Network - a way to secure your IP address by giving you temporarily a new IP. That means hackers and online providers are not able to see where the signal is coming from. The background is that hackers might be able to access your home network through your IP address or collect personal data.

Hackers are searching for wallet connections to find the user. A wallet has a unique pattern of small data transactions with the blockchain - those could be detected and could identify your IP.

A VPN is distracting potential hackers from your assets and makes it hard for them to allocate your position and network. Even though VPNs are a good additional security measure that does not mean that you and your assets are at risk if you are not using a VPN.

2FA

2FA or two-factor-authenticator is a must have! Regardless of the exchange you use, you should always enable the 2FA. The google authenticator, for example, is an application which generates a new password every 20 seconds and is linked to your account.

(This software is based on a TOTP protocol, meaning Temporary One Time Password. The most famous and

secure app is the "Google Authenticator". We highly recommend using it instead of SMS 2FA.)

Conclusion

As the world becomes more digitalised day by day, data security is one of the most burning issues. Cryptocurrencies are a considerable part of this change; therefore, it is vital for every user to be an expert in security measures.

Besides all those rules, there is one thing that could reduce the risk, and it is called "understatement". Even if you own Cryptoassets over 1 million, you should never talk about it. Understatement can save you from robbery, hackers and false friends.

Last but not least, it is essential that indifferent which wallet you decide to use, always tell someone how to access your coins. Cryptocurrencies still have a considerable uncertainty ahead of them, and currently, most people do not know much about it. Therefore, even though this is something most people do not think about, you should always be aware of the possibility of dying or losing the ability to access your funds. It will be a significant loss if you have a considerable amount of assets, which your family cannot access because they do not know how. Take some time to create a "what if" plan. The positive side effect is that you might arouse the interest of your partner, children, parents or whomever.

Mining

We were talking about mining at an earlier stage of this book already. Mining is the process of validating transactions, by solving difficult cryptographic tasks through trying (to create consensus within the network). In order to find the solution of a block, the miner is guessing several solutions until he sees one.

(This process is defined by the mining difficulty and the hash-rate, which we will explain in the following segment.)

In PoW, solving this task requires graphics and lots of electricity. It is compulsory that mining is creating costs (at least opportunity costs) because otherwise, the incentives of making false validations would be too high.

Mining difficulty

The mining difficulty describes, how hard it is to find the right solution to be able to verify (mine) the block. Every Cryptocurrency adjusts this difficulty in another way; therefore, the difficulty and its process can vary.

All the Cryptocurrencies based on the Proof of Work algorithm increase their mining difficulty from time to time. The reason for this is that usually the more blocks are mined, the more miners there are searching for solutions. This means that if the difficulty stayed the same, the blocks would be mined too fast.

(You can visualise it the following way: Think of a lock with numbers. To find a block, you need to unlock this lock. First, it has three unknown quantities, and all of the other miners are trying to open it by striving (1000 possible solutions). With an increasing mining difficulty, the lock gains another number so the miner has to find the solutions out of 4 spots (10,000 possible solutions).)

(If you remember the chapter about proof of work, we were explaining that the reward for mining a block is reducing itself as well. Connected to the increasing mining difficulty, this is the reason why many experts are saying that Bitcoin mining is not profitable anymore.)

Hash-rate

The hash-rate specifies how many solutions can be guessed (mostly per second). It can be described in MH/s (mega hash) up to TH/s (terra hash).

(Back to our example with the lock. The hash-rate describes, how many solutions the miner can try per second.)

How can I mine?

There are several ways of mining, but remember they all depend on the performance of your mining device.

CPU Mining

CPU mining, or mining with your computer, is one of the most convenient but least profitable ways of mining a Cryptocurrency. A better-quality computer can reach a hash-rate of around 25 MH/s, which is not sufficient enough to compete with mining pools that reach hash-rates of TH/s (billions of solutions).

GPU Mining

Most of the private people who are mining are using GPU mining that describes the usage of graphics to mine. One good graphic can alone reach a hash-rate of around 30 MH/s and uses far less energy than a computer. This is the reason why so many gaming graphics were sold out because they were attractive for miners.

ASIC Mining

ASIC mining describes the usage of specially produced equipment. These are computers with the lone purpose of mining, and they are unable to do anything else but mine. This is the most common way for most mining farms, due to their high performance.

If you want to know more about mining and the possibility of earning money with it, you can check various calculators on the internet. From our perspective mining with small setups is not profitable anymore if you target big currencies. The only logical ways would be investing in a mining pool or finding small, undervalued market caps, which offer greater rewards.

Initial Coin Offerings (ICOs)

The term initial coin offering is based on the initial public offering from the share market. Indeed, there are many similarities between an ICO and an IPO. An IPO is an event, where a company issues their shares and offers them to selected trades. Those shares later start circulating in the stock markets.

(Usually, it is tough for a "normal" person to participate in IPO, because the shares are first offered to investment banks and then to the public.)

An ICO, on the other hand, is available for everyone, and there mostly is no exclusion. (US citizens or citizens of other countries may be excluded.) The only thing that could prohibit a person is the minimum amount you have to spend. Usually, ICO has a couple of other distinctions to an IPO.

A significant difference is that while a share is a piece of the company and with that piece, you have the right to see what the company is doing with your money. A coin is nothing like that. With owning the coin, you do not have any share of the company behind the ICO. Because of the missing regulatory, an investor can only hope that the team is working responsibly with its funds.

By participating in an ICO, you usually get a bonus if you buy in early stages of the ICO.

To be able to participate in an ICO, it is essential that you read the details of the participation. For example, you cannot send the funds for the ICO from an exchange - you need to send them from a wallet which is approved by the team.

When buying coins in an ICO, you should be aware of the fact that there is no regulatory oversight. That means, there is a danger of scams, but do not be afraid - we will teach you how to distinguish good from bad ICOs and everything else relevant in the investment section.

Some ICOs might as well have a "whitelist". The whitelist is collecting participants of the ICO in advance. This is usually done by very popular ICOs which have limited participation possibilities. The soft and hard cap limits the coins distributed. The hard cap describes the absolute limit of money being raised, while the soft cap is the target that must be reached for the team to start working (it is lower than the hard cap). In case the soft cap is not matched, the funds are usually returned. If the hard cap is filled and there are other investors transferring funds, those will be returned as well.

(Scams could be an exception. If you do not receive funds back or no value in return, it is a major red flag for further investments in this currency.)

Last but not least there is a phrase called "gas war". This happens in an ICO where the demand is enormous. As we learned already, transactions are processed by miners ordered by the transaction fees. To secure coins in the ICO, many people offer extremely high fees to have their orders processed first. This betting war is called gas war.

If you do not know how to use all this information to develop a sound investment strategy, do not panic, we will discuss everything you need to know in our investment section.

What coins are there?

Currently there are above 1,500 Cryptocurrencies (March 2018) and rising. Many of them follow a certain "mission", while others appear to be scam, with no real added value. In this chapter we will have a look at what types of coins are out there and how to classify them, based on their technology as well as their purpose.

Furthermore, this chapter will consolidate your basic understanding of Cryptocurrencies, what is essential in order to be a successful Crypto-Trader. *(The broad differentiation is taken from Angus Cepka and will be supplemented by our subdivision.)*

Cryptocurrencies

This topic may sound very broad, and in a way, every coin/token is a Cryptocurrency, but we want to stress an important distinction. Cryptocurrencies are coins/tokens which function as a substitution for FIAT money (EUR, USD...). Therefore, only currencies which are intended to be used as a payment method are listed in this category.

In this category of cryptos, we can distinguish between "Asset storage/currency", "Privacy Coins" and "Internet of Things".

Asset storage/currency

We will start with the "asset storage/currency". This category includes amongst others, for example, Bitcoin, Litecoin and Tether. Many people stress that due to its scalability issues, Bitcoin will never be used as common currency. Therefore, some experts stress that Bitcoin will become the storage of value - the "digital gold".

Litecoin is an example of a currency which can be used on an everyday basis due to its high scalability and low fees.

Tether, on the other hand, is an example of a Cryptocurrency which is backed by FIAT money. This can be compared to the USD until the 1970's, which has been backed by gold. (In theory, a US-dollar bill was a security certificate supported by the value of gold and silver.)

Privacy Coins

The second category of Cryptocurrencies is called "privacy coins". Privacy coins are currencies which are constructed with the purpose of anonymous payments. The most famous are Monero (XMR), Zcash (ZEC) and Verge (XVG).

Distinctive for this group of currencies is that those coins usually do not have a rich list. *(A rich list is a list of the wealthiest addresses. For example, you can see which address is holding the most BTC here: https://bitinfocharts.com/top-100-richest-bitcoin-addresses.html).*

Furthermore, these coins can be used to transmit secret information of personal or business manner. (Remember, usually it is possible to read each block of the blockchain and see its content.)

Internet of Things Coins (IoT)

The last category we want to discuss here is the "IoT currencies" (Internet of things).

As the exploration of the IoT technology continues to succeed, this part of Cryptocurrencies may become a vital part of your daily life. The most popular currency here is IOTA, which is cooperating with a couple of the largest companies in the world such as Bosch, Volkswagen and others.

You might remember from the previous chapter that the main characteristics of the Tangle technology were the unlimited scalability and the lack of transaction fees. This makes it ideal to use it with the internet of things technology.

(Imagine you drive your car into a car park and it automatically pays its fees. Your fridge might recognise the lack of some ingredients. Or your mobile phone is paying its costs. All of these transactions would run automatically and without any fees and need to intervene.)

This category is a continually growing part of the Cryptoworld.

Platforms

One of the most versatile fields are the so-called platforms. Cryptocurrencies which provide such a platform are real multi-talents and highly complex. The most famous representative in this field is undoubtedly Ethereum, the second largest Cryptocurrency out there (March 2018). Besides Ethereum there are popular alternatives such as NEO (the Asian Ethereum), Cardano (ADA) and others.

These platforms have different adaptability possibilities. The primary intention is to provide a decentralised basis for applications, which can be built on top of the blockchain. If you remember the difference between a coin and a token, we have talked about coins having their blockchain and tokens using the existing platforms to be built on top. To make a transaction with a token such as EOS (currently the largest token of Ethereum), the transmitter needs to pay a fee in the underlying currency.

(The Cryptocurrency NEO is, as we already mentioned before, a Proof of Stake coin. The interest payments are made in "Gas", which is needed by tokens built on NEO to verify the transactions.)

The possible adaptions are widespread, to only name a few, this kind of technology perfectly suits the demand of the economy in the form of smart contracts, business ecosystems and many others.

Adaptability Coins

One of the most considerable disadvantages in the Cryptoworld is for sure the lack of adaption. As we learnt already the blockchain cannot be changed easily, only with a fork. This is the reason why many new coins have to create a new blockchain. While the new blockchain is not compatible with the older ones, this raises a significant issue for the old blockchains.

(The "Tezos Position Paper" by L.M Goodman from 2014 gives an excellent example: Think Cryptocurrencies were like smartphones. Every now and then a new smartphone is released with new features and technologies. In general, the old smartphone can still be used and is compatible with the new smartphone. But what if the old smartphone wouldn't be able to interact with the new one? The value of the old smartphone would decrease rapidly.)

This is a great problem in the current Crypto-Market. Currently, there is only one coin trying to solve this issue named TEZOS. It is a blockchain, which can be adapted. The changes need to be approved by the stakeholder of this coin, which is run by a "delegated Proof of Stake" algorithm.

Bridge coins

Another subdivision we want to discuss is "bridge coins" or coins which provide the "smart bridge" technology. These coins such as ARK, can create a connection between different blockchains. This is doable with atomic swaps as well, but those are only possible if the underlying blockchain has the same protocol. With ARK every blockchain can be connected such as Ethereum, Bitcoin and Lisk.

(The practical implication could be sending the information of a smart contract you want to run over the ARK network to the Ethereum network, without possessing ETHER.)

Utility Tokens

The Cryptoworld takes many ideas from current technologies and tries to improve those. The central part of every person's daily life are applications, which control and steer many things. Utility tokens are the equivalent to these applications (APIs), as they are Cryptocurrencies which offer a specific service.

Many projects in the Cryptoworld are tokens based on another platform such as Ethereum (erc20 tokens). A utility token is nothing else than a tool that serves as "fuel" for the underlying technology.

That means a utility token has a specific task on the Blockchain such as paying transaction fees or providing entrance to a service on the blockchain. A utility token can contain voting rights as well.

This category is not designed as an investment, but this does not mean they will not increase in value nor that they have a weaker purpose. Investing in utility tokens means investing in solutions, while the primary goal of the project is to grow and improve the system, not to increase value.

Those utility coins could have very different purposes, such as strategic backgrounds or others. One example could be ADX which functions as an intermediary of companies and consumers.

(ADX is an application which aims to revolutionise the advertisement world. The system focuses on a better advertising placement and plans to take the place of the intermediary so that the advertiser can directly publish its

ads without the need of a marketing company. BAT is following a similar path.)

Another solution could be the data storage, which is solved by for example Siacoin. The system provides an encrypted, decentralised storage network, which is a way to rent the available room on your computer in return for coins. (Dropbox with personal providers.)

This method of creating storage is already described as the future of cloud storage and could become a real competitor for Dropbox, Google, Amazon and so on. It provides not only a higher security standard but also it undercuts the prices of the large competitors by far.

Another exciting and rapidly growing part of utility tokens is the DEXes (decentralised exchanges). You probably heard the media talking about a major hack and millions of dollars being stolen. This is a significant threat from a traditional exchange, and a decentralised one can reduce it.

A DEX is an open source marketplace, where nobody controls the exchange and the user is holding its coins directly and not the exchange. That means it is far more secure and you have a high degree of anonymity.

While offering a couple of advantages, this type of exchange has some downsides as well. It is far more inconvenient. Things like credit card usage, trading tools, and often low trading volume are some disadvantages of a DEX. Exceptions are the significant DEXes which have a high trading volume and offer trading tools, such as graphs.

(Currently, Idex for ETH and Switcheo for NEO are the most popular DEXes.)

By reading this, you have probably recognised that this section of utility tokens appears to be endless and indeed it encompasses most of the Cryptocurrencies out there. As we mentioned before we only want to give you an insight on how to distinguish utility tokens within that group, therefore we are not going to name further ones. As soon as you start looking at specific coins, you will see that there are other categories like gambling coins (STOX) and many more.

Cryptosecurities

While most of the coins at the end of 2017 were utility tokens, there is another emerging group of coins called Cryptosecurities.

Cryptosecurities are, contrary to utility tokens, backed by external and tradable assets so that this category can be compared to shares. As we mentioned before in the ICO chapter, typically possessing a coin does not result in the ownership of the company behind the currency. Cryptosecurities are the one main exception, as they entitle the holders to ownership rights.

Cryptocurrencies are very speculative, and often the investor can have some influence on their price. With Cryptosecurities that influence is non-existent as the value depends solely on the company's performance and its equity. Because Cryptosecurities are backed by some assets or value such as a company, the profitability of the investment is dependent on the development and not pure marketing speculation, as it often takes place in Cryptocurrencies.

In April 2018, there are only a few Cryptosecurities as it still is an emerging category. A new player on the market called Polymath is working at this "issue" and offers an easy way to create security tokens. Polymath functions as a marketplace and platform to issue tokens.

This differentiation could become very important because in theory security tokens are controlled by the Securities and Exchange Commission (SEC). That makes it possible for financial institutions to trade their shares on the blockchain or issue further shares based on a Cryptosecurity. Being regulated and backed by real assets or services is an utterly revolutionising idea and we are optimistic that this category will be one of the big gainers in 2018.

Hybrids

There are dozens of hybrids out there which are following different courses and do not fit in one of the groups mentioned before. Hybrids are an emerging group of coins, due to the reason that there are so many other currencies out there and the competition became more diversified.

It can be an advantage as well as a disadvantage if a Cryptocurrency is ambivalent; therefore, this group cannot be determined better or worse than the others.

Why should we use Cryptocurrencies?

All these technological features look to revolutionise, but what are they good for? This is a question many people ask themselves. Unfortunately, many experts on Cryptocurrencies have no relation to the economy and therefore, miss the opportunity of talking about Cryptocurrencies. In this part of the book, we are going to talk about several industries which could rely on Cryptocurrencies as the basis for new markets, processes and so on.

Taking the potential influence on the economy into consideration, we will be able to analyse why Cryptocurrencies might be a revolutionary invention, or why it is not suitable for specific industries.

After talking about the basic functions and technologies behind Bitcoin and co., you might agree that the invention of the blockchain could be the start of something huge. Before we start with our analysis, we want to emphasise that it is not the purpose of this book to tell you in which industries you should invest or which might have the most promising future. It is about learning how to evaluate sector and offering a different point of view.

To revise the most important things from the previous chapter, we will do a little repetition.

Repetition

- The blockchain cannot be hacked and is, therefore, one of the most secure data processes in the world. (What quantum computers could do and if they are a real threat, will be discussed in the "Facts" chapter).

- Everyone can view every transaction or content which has been validated in a block. In addition to that, it is not possible to change any of the collected information.

- Transactions will be approved day and night, no matter where are they located in the world. Furthermore, these transactions usually take a lot less than they would if they were done by banks and probably cost less as well.

- There are platform networks, which allow users to write and run smart contracts on the network.

- The adaptability chances are nearly endless, and the current market is rapidly expanding.

This was a very short summarise, but you have to have these points in mind while thinking about the several industries.

Smart Contracts

We mentioned the term smart contracts several times in this book, and it is time to tell you what a smart contract is or could be.

A smart contract is not as complicated as it may sound. It is an agreement between two people which is not viewed and controlled by an intermediary, only the system. That means if a party breaches that contract, the blockchain automatically executes the arrangements (which were agreed before) or enforces any other obligation which has been added to the contract. A smart contract could look like this:

1) Two (anonymous) parties agree on leasing contract for one's flat. Everyone in the blockchain can view the contract itself. (In this contract are the parties named by the public addresses and not by their names.)

2) The 1st of each month is the payment day; therefore, the contract executes a transaction from the tenant to the landlord

3) Regulators can check if the contract is legal, without interfering with the privacy of both participants.

What if...

1) If the tenant does not pay the rent, the apartment could be locked automatically.

2) If the landlord made false promises or the flat is not accessible, the blockchain automatically refunds the money.

Making smart contracts supports each unit in an equal way; therefore, no site has an advantage due to lawyers or others.

Vitalik Buterin, the founder of Ethereum, explained it like this:

"In a smart contract approach, an asset or currency is transferred into a program and the program runs this code and at some point, it automatically validates a condition and it automatically determines whether the asset should go to one person or back to the other person, or whether it should be immediately refunded to the person who sent it or some combination thereof. In the meantime, the decentralized ledger also stores and replicates the document which gives it a certain security and immutability."

Automotive Industry

One of the largest industries interested in smart contracts is the automotive industry. It is not surprising that nearly all of the large car manufacturers such as VW (IOTA), BMW (VeChain), Daimler (own crypto) and others are already working with Cryptocurrencies.

In 2017 car manufacturers worldwide sold over 80,000,000 cars (new cars only), while on average nearly every second a car is leased *(meaning that around 40 million cars were leased in 2017).*

This part of the automotive industry could process all of their leasing contracts over a blockchain like Ethereum and gain greater control over payments and at the same time cut jobs, which were not needed anymore.

But this is only a small part of what could become possible. Volkswagen is one of IOTA's partners and together they are aiming to revolutionise the car payments. The ultimate aim is to have an autonomous car which can make microtransactions with the parking lot, toll stations or tickets, without the need to take any action.

(If you park into a parking lot, the car is paying the exact time you parked on that spot not more and not less. If you enter a toll road, the station can accurately ·charge according to the length or duration you travelled on the way. This is possible because Cryptocurrencies like IOTA have no to minimal transaction fees; therefore, small transactions can be submitted.)

A startup called CarVertical, for example, tries to revolutionise the second-hand market for cars. The idea is to save each vehicle on the blockchain and keep the blockchain updated about the condition of the motor, the kilometres travelled, accidents and so on to prevent criminal manipulations on second-hand cars. This technology could have a massive influence on the industry as a whole, as there are further adaptability possibilities regarding new cars.

Banks

Yes, banks could use and work with Cryptocurrencies as well. Many people assume that if Cryptocurrencies succeed, Banks will "die" and the money distribution will be revolutionised. In fact, that could be a way, but to be honest, it is doubtful that banks will disappear due to several reasons which we will not discuss in this chapter. We want to focus on how banks and other financial institutions could benefit from Cryptocurrencies and the underlying technology.

Coins related to the banking system, are quite popular. You might have heard about Ripple, as this is a highly polarising coin. Besides Ripple, there are a couple of Cryptocurrencies in the market with similar possibilities for banks, such as "Stellar Lumens" (XLM).

The most significant advantages are the cost benefits. One international transaction can take up to 4 business days and costs around 2-5% plus additional costs.

Banks are required to have nostro and vostro accounts (ours and yours) for interbank transfers such as international transactions.

(In short, a nostro account is an account by bank A at bank B. A vostro account is the same, from the perspective of bank B. To make an international transaction (different currencies), banks are required to request a transaction on their nostro account. This is connected to high risk due to inflation and exchange rates. In addition to that, billions and trillions of dollars are unavailable and stored in those accounts.)

Ripple does not solve these issues entirely but can reduce the costs drastically. Using the Ripple Network, banks could not only process transactions a lot faster, but they would also cost a fraction of the amount. Another benefit would be the reduction of staff which is needed to process the transactions.

The clue is, Ripple provides the liquidity for the different accounts on an on-demand basis. This system is called xRapid and uses the Ripple Coin as the primary currency.

Another system provided by Ripple Labs is xCurrent, which is already in testing by Santander, UBS, American Express, UniCredit, BBVA and many others.

(xCurrent is an application which allows end to end transactions within seconds. Ripple estimates that they can save up to 33% of the costs.

xRapid provides the liquidity for the banks so that they do not have to give nostro and vostro accounts.

xVia is the last piece of the puzzle and is the connecting interface between xCurrent and xRapid.)

It is up to the banks, whether they use only xCurrent or the system as a whole. The most likely scenario is that banks are going to use the Ripple network (xCurrent) and create their digital currency for liquidity.

The old banking system could be revolutionised, but not replaced. Instead of fighting each other the best way would be to work together.

In this industry, the potential of Cryptocurrencies is enormous, but not as an investment itself. Many banks and businesses avoid Cryptocurrencies because they are very volatile. Therefore, banks and credit card providers prefer using the network with their currency (USD, EUR etc.).

(According to Ripple as an investment (!), many people are buying the currency without knowing the disadvantages of it. As we will see learn in the investment section, it is essential to know how many coins are distributed and how many coins are held by the founders. In Ripple's case, the founder has around 30% of the total supply and would, therefore, be able to manipulate the value by himself. Additionally, Ripple is not limited, and in case there will be banks working with Ripple, they will probably not use the coin, but only the network.)

Social Media

The third industry which could be significantly influenced by Cryptocurrencies is the social media. Here, many different types such as messengers, influencers or communities could change towards a decentralised system.

As for messengers, a couple of the largest providers already created and published a Cryptocurrency. The messenger Kik (over 300 million users) launched its Cryptocurrency at the end of 2017 called KIN.

The messenger Telegram (200 million users) is currently offering their coin through an ICO called TON. It will be based on a PoS system and will tackle not only messages but also money transactions. One of the big advantages for Telegram is that it is already the main messenger for Crypto-groups and financial context.

Influencers are the most current group of marketers, which are an essential part of today's social media. For those of you who have never heard of influencers, it is a "job" in which famous people (people with many followers in various platforms such as Instagram, Facebook, Snapchat...) advertise products through their channels.

The cryptosphere could profoundly influence this part of online marketing. Here, the companies can create a task (for example position product xy), and influencer can fulfil this task by creating content. Instead of creating marketing campaigns top to bottom, currencies such as "Friendz" create a peer to peer communication – using the powerful word of mouth marketing.

Regarding the communities, the Cryptoworld offers many different and exciting possibilities. A project is called LBRY Credits is one of many Cryptocurrencies concerned with the distribution and publication of content, such as books, music, blogs and so on. The project wants to create an exchange of data without the typical intermediary who takes away the most substantial part of the money.

Another already popular application is called STEEM. It was initially founded to be a site where it is possible to publish any written content with some benefits to it, as users can reward writers who did an excellent job with STEEM coins.

A lot of other exciting projects are out there, but we will stop at this point as the examples should be enough.

We can conclude, that social media has the potential of being heavily influenced by Cryptocurrencies, not only because of the popularity. As you might have heard on the news, Facebook was accused of using their user's data against their will. We would not be surprised if Facebook were not the only one doing this. Cryptocurrencies could increase user's safety significantly and secure them against social media providers abusing their data.

(Facebook is about to start its research on Cryptocurrencies. Mark Zuckerberg, the founder of Facebook, has already said that he is interested in developing his own.)

Healthcare

The adaption possibilities in the healthcare industry are enormous and highly discussed amongst many companies such as Deloitte, IBM and others. Health care information is one of the most sensitive information in the world; therefore, the demand for a more secure and private structure is very high.

(One model could be hospitals and doctors track everything as they used to, but instead of saving them locally, they would keep the information on the blockchain. This information is sent to the blockchain just like a transaction, meaning you cannot see who this information belongs to. Once the data is saved on the blockchain, the information could be used for studies, research and others without violating personal interests, due to the anonymity. If a patient needs to attend a doctor, he can provide all his personal information with his private key.)

The result would be that the patient has all his medical data and can decide who has access to it. This avoids the violation of personal data and secures the data against natural catastrophes.

Other benefits could be the prevention of drug abuse, when institutions and doctors can see who received which medication to which extent. Smart contracts could supervise the data access, in case a patient is seeing another doctor, but wants his first doctor to know about everything. All kinds of research such as genomics could be supported due to large data pools, and it creates the option of enabling an "early warning system".

As you can see, everyone could benefit from a blockchain based health care system. The change towards big data pools where millions of personal data are saved has already begun. The question whether it is better to keep them at a central place or in an unhackable blockchain will surely be a big topic soon, as the development continues. Already existing currencies include Medicalchain or Medibloc (April 2018).

Energy

Another industry everyone has to rely on is the energy sector. Similar to the previous examples, this sector is already working on solutions, and a couple of interesting projects were established.

The most significant advantage here is the elimination of the intermediary, meaning consumers do not need an energy provider to exchange green energy between one another.

(Imagine you have solar panels on your roof and create 300KWH a day, but use only 200KWH. Right now, the difference is sent to the energy supplier in return for a small remuneration or saved in a battery. In both ways, lots of energy is lost. With the blockchain technology, you can give the electricity directly to your neighbour and receive a considerable remuneration. The best thing yet - you do not have to do anything, because smart contracts are running the transactions by themselves.)

Electricity could be dealt as a real asset, meaning smart contracts are selling the power automatically to the highest bid. This would avoid substantial price differences between electricity providers and create a fair system of usage.

In 2016 there has been a pilot program called "Brooklyn Microgrid", which provided an app to deal excessive electricity within their neighbourhood.

Currently, many Cryptocurrencies are working on solutions such as MWAT, POWR and others. It will probably take more years to develop to provide a mass solution, but the fact that renewable energies are gaining popularity continuously offers good foundation.

Supply chain networks

Living in a globalised system with comprehensive capitalism, supply chain networks are one of the most important fields for globally operating companies. Companies like Walmart have a highly developed system which allows them to save costs and maximise profits in the best way possible.

Modern supply chain networks are highly complex as they often require several independent systems in many countries. For global players it is normal to send their goods throughout the whole world for producing, shipping, selling and so on. These goods enter different tariff zones and pass several boards before arriving at the shop, ready to be sold. Due to this complexity, it becomes challenging to keep track of all movements and contact points.

A solution could be a decentralised network synchronising all the data at once, to increase the company's abilities. The headquarters could easily access all the data in the supply chain, and payments could be made automatically. Currencies which are exploring these opportunities are Origintrail, Vechain or Wabi.

Another approach to this technology is improving the record of goods. Today, it is imperative for many people to know where the food or clothes are coming from. This could be another important solution the blockchain can provide. Cloths registered in one place (the origin) cannot be manipulated afterwards, once it is on the blockchain. That means customers can check where the clothes were produced. You might say that this is already possible, but what about cars or more complex products which are for example MADE IN GERMANY? Are those goods 100% made in Germany or just a certain percentage of them is? These questions could be answered by checking the blockchain. A provider here would be TE-Food, which is working on food solutions, namely a "farm-to-table traceability solution."

We can conclude that this section has, similar to all the other application fields, endless possibilities. Due to the strong economy behind it (Walmart, Target, H&M...), it could become a real game-changer, and it remains to be seen in which extent it will influence the economy we know.

B2B

In general, many companies could use Cryptocurrencies for B2B or Business to Business solutions. Most of these transactions are made on a regular basis and therefore consume many resources, such as auditors, accountants and so on.

In the telecommunication industry, it is normal that some providers use telephone poles of their competitors to provide reception. Usually, these providers rent capacities and pay compensation on a regular basis. But there are also cases, where the provider has to make a payment for each call.

Smart contracts would be able to solve this "issue", by analysing the consumed data and transmitting payments automatically.

All companies could benefit from the technology, small or large. However, this technology is currently only interesting for large companies such as Bosch, Daimler, Google, Apple and so on.

Conclusion

We can conclude that there is nearly no industry in the whole world which could not be affected by the Cryptocurrency revolution. There are millions of adaption possibilities just waiting to be explored.

In fact, the research expenses on blockchain and co have never been as high as currently. Almost every large company is investigating the technology to determine potential applications.

Only time will tell, whether and how this technology will evolve. But the future is, despite all the bad noise, very promising.

Part 2

Fundamental Analysis

In this part of the book, we will present how to do proper research on ICOs and coins which are already on the market. We will do that by evaluating the project as well as methods used to find the best of them. At the end of this chapter, you will be able to conduct an in-depth analysis of any coin. In addition to that, you will be able to spot scams and understand the influence fundamentals should have on your investment decisions. For this segment, we will use "FA" as an abbreviation for Fundamental Analysis.

The role of Fundamental Analysis in crypto investing

Before we dig deeper into the research itself, we will explain why it is essential to do research in the first place and how important the fundamentals are for investments. In a market where most projects do not have a prototype, and real research does not back most investment decisions, the question that arises is: Is it really necessary to understand coin's fundamentals? The answer to that depends on the time frame a person will trade on.

If there is no product to evaluate a project's basis, the price of that coin often results from a mixture of current developments and speculations about its future potential. The market is not rational when it comes to evaluating the progress – very often coins with a working product and sealed partnerships are worth millions of dollars less than platforms with nothing to show besides a White Paper. A few team members working previously in a famous company, like Microsoft, might be more valuable to investors than several real use cases a coin possesses. A well-known advisor, like John McAfee, is often worth more than an experienced development team. We could go on like this forever, but the conclusion is simple – the market cap of the project is almost never a fair representation of the coin's value. So, you might ask what influences the price so much in those projects that are far less developed than their competitors? The answer to that is also the reason why a lot of people in the Cryptocurrency world do not believe FA works – hype.

We have seen many coins during the past alt seasons that were changing lives with their growth despite (often unfair) scam accusations or lacklustre technology (DigiByte, Tron and Verge come to mind as the classical examples of all-time pumps). It did not make a difference that Tron was accused of copying parts of its White Paper from other projects or that DigiByte became a running joke with it "being very fast". They were going up the value rankings, surpassing projects which are far superior in their utility but which lacked more exposure. How is it possible that a worse coin has more hype around it? There are many different reasons for this:

- The idea is easy to understand and to market. Verge is a privacy coin – easy. Enigma, on the other hand, is a privacy protocol utilising secret contracts – not so much (and it is the most accessible description we found for it).

- There is a big community behind it. Very often when coin experiences a rapid growth (as Verge did from 1 sat to over 1600), it is natural that the project gains a large group of supporters. In many cases, the community can have a more significant influence than any other possible partnership or milestone reached. People around the coin provide the word-of-mouth marketing unmatchable with any different kind of promotion and it is extraordinarily powerful since the people are invested in the project as well.

- There is a highlight point inside of the project, whether it is Tim Draper on the investors' page or a partnership with PwC. People very often tend to focus on these points while shilling a project because that implicates a sign of value and therefore, creates hype. Most people never go deeper than the main page of the coin's website, so it is crucial that a project has a unique selling point to create better exposure. A general rule that explains it - price is based on speculation, and hype fuels speculation.

- There is an important event incoming that builds up a lot of hype around the project. Meanwhile, the competitors are steadily delivering results on the side without any critical catalysts coming up as they already possess a working product.

How important is fundamental analysis in decision making? As we mentioned earlier, it depends on the time frame. If you are planning to make a short-term trade (few days maximum) based solely on fundamentals, you will quickly become disappointed. Short-term moves are based on events and good TA setups - a strong team or a working product will have no influence here. For a mid-term trade (few weeks), it becomes a little trickier. The move still depends on upcoming news, but because of a more extended trading period, knowledge of fundamentals can provide potential drawbacks. If the team had a history of not delivering on time or if you are aware of some FUD that might start circulating, it helps to decide how significant a position in that coin should be, based on the risk associated with it.

Lastly, the long-term trade, which is the primary time frame where FA works. The in-depth analysis allows you to understand how big the potential is for the project during the next few months and beyond. This is where you decide if the coin is worth putting into cold storage (remember chapter wallets) and storing it for a longer time. All elements matter such as the idea, team, coin metrics, development time frame. On that basis, you decide if the project will be able to reach its goals, generate hype and most importantly if the coin itself will be able to gain value over time.

To sum it up, fundamentals are essential when evaluating a coin in the long-term. For shorter trade time frames, it is important to understand what is behind the coins, but the focus should be on the current development and events surrounding it. All projects which are in an early development stage and outside the bigger audience, are extremely easy to be manipulated by Cryptocurrency influencers (like YouTuber Suppoman, who notoriously causes price spikes when he talks about specific coins to his numerous followers). That is until the cryptosphere becomes more mature and coins will be evaluated not based on speculation but real development.

Finding coins

The age-old question, how do I find a gem - the next Bitcoin/Ethereum. Unfortunately, the answer to this will not satisfy most of you. Whatever method we are going to choose, it always takes a lot of time and effort to find that next great opportunity. The reason for this is that the key to success in finding a coin that will go times 10, 20, 50 or even 100 is to be in it as early as possible. Of course, it needs to have strong fundamentals that would allow it to grow outside of its yet tiny market cap, but it will not matter that much if you do not catch it at the bottom. Every trader has their way of doing the research, so we will try to describe every method we have come across so far and we think is successful.

CoinMarketCap

The most basic but still one of the best ways of finding undervalued coins is looking at the website CoinMarketCap.com. The process is very simple. You go through hundreds of coins, do a quick research on each one of them until you find something worth doing a more in-depth check. The trick is to know what to look for.

To find coins with a low market cap, you need to filter them according to their current market cap and trading volume. The first metric depends on the overall capitalisation.

(In the summer of 2017 low cap could be counted anywhere below 250K dollars, while in April 2018 coins below 1M were already considered extreme by some.)

Once you get the coins below that level, you should filter out those with little to no trading volume - this should save you some time on checking probably dead coins. Besides, counting on a community resurrection is never a sound strategy. In addition to that, from the chosen currencies of low cap and moderate volume (few % in comparison to the cap is enough) you can check the circulating to total supply ratio before going deeper into the project. Too much of a difference here could mean a big "premine" which often brings the risk of being dumped on by the developer.

Some coins are mined before being listed on an exchange, or the mining process is exclusive for specific users. That means those users can mine coins in large stakes before anyone else can. This is a scam coin issue because the developers can sell large stakes and dump the project.

That is, however, not always the case so if you are willing to check the reasoning behind such disparity, feel free to do so as it might turn out to be rewarding. Same rules apply to any other coin-listing platform out there, such as Coinlib (we will list CoinMarketCap alternatives at the end of this book).

For more established coins we would highly suggest checking out daily updates of recently added coins – it is a section that might not give you the earliest entry since it takes time for some coins to get listed on CoinMarketCap, but it can get you entry before the majority recognises the opportunity.

Always be careful when investing in this category. Microcaps that were mined and traded before getting listed very often are dumped once they receive more liquidity. In the same time, previously unknown ICOs that just got listed might provide an excellent opportunity to buy before others realise their potential. Regardless of the outcome, being listed is an important exposure period which should be tracked and possibly played for short-term swing or an occasion for long-term entry.

Twitter

This method is trickier since it also involves bias of investors towards specific coins; therefore, it is harder to find a rational valuation of the project. The point is to see a small shill of a coin that you have never heard of before, preferably from an unpopular account *(by another investment rule: if big guys are talking about a coin/investment, it is no longer an early entry).*

One opportunity to find those shills are within Twitter threads of bigger profiles, whether it is a recently popular "shill me coins" thread or just a regular post that somebody thought would be a great place to promote their investment. Getting first recognition for a very young or undervalued project is extremely hard to do; therefore, investors try to gain the attention of famous traders, because they can enhance the chance of increasing the coin's value. As much as everybody hates those people jumping into every topic, shilling coins without being asked for it can be a great opportunity.

At the end of this book, we are listing many traders that are worth following in our opinion. This can be your foundation that will help you decide who should be added to this list next.

Bitcointalk

Bitcointalk was and still is one of the most important Cryptocurrency forums, and it is vital for all crypto-related projects. It is not as popular right now as it has been for coins to communicate through this forum with their investors (the communication shifted to telegram) because many do not even bother to update their [ANN] in there anymore. That does not change the fact that there still is no better place to catch a project that appeared on the market 5 minutes before you discovered it.

It does not matter if it is an ICO or a fair-launched new PoW coin. Everything begins with creating an [ANN] and that gives you the earliest possible entry there is - way before CoinMarketCap, and social media do. Researching Bitcointalk is usually connected with operating on insufficient information about the project comparing to already established coins, but that is why it is also more rewarding for those willing to take the additional risk (by buying the unproven).

To start researching Bitcointalk, open the website and enter the Announcements page in the Alternate Cryptocurrencies category. From that moment you are on your own. Go through all the new threads and see if there is anything worth an early entry.

Exchanges

This one is overlooked because most people trade on big exchanges like Binance or Bittrex, but there are dozens of other good exchanges that list coins a lot more frequently than those two giants. Not many coins go straight away to the most significant exchange in the world, more often they advance from small, low volume ones up to middle-tier exchanges like KuCoin to finally land on top platforms. Apart from merely going through all the listed coins that you are not aware off (you will find out more about the best places to do that in the latter part of the book), it is also important to look for projects with tiny volume. Usually when few main coins are gathering most of the exchange's volume, once the hype ends, the investors are looking for other opportunities on the same platform (so that they do not have to withdraw their money) giving a chance to other coins to pump as well. Do not be discouraged by the low liquidity in a currency that has a stable price action – small volume is where you buy, high volume is where you sell. That is, of course, if you are playing to maximise your gains, which often requires investing before the confirmation of the new uptrend.

Upcoming events

Probably the most common way to find a good investment opportunity is to focus on upcoming events. With websites like Coinmarketcal.com, it is a lot easier to go through coins with some forthcoming announcements or launches to ride the hype preluding to it.

This is mostly a short-term strategy, and it should be approached with caution. As we will see in the Technical Analysis chapter, the news is usually already priced in, meaning that, often, the most significant price growth has already occurred. However, since in the cryptosphere even small events like roadmap releases have a big impact on the generated hype, it is common to ride along with it and sell moments before the actual release/launch. By the general rule "Buy the rumour, sell the news", you do not want to be left in the project with most investors planning to sell their coins. Just make sure that the news is significant (product launch, token burn, White Paper release) before investing in it – it must be an event that will generate a lot of noise around the community.

Now is the moment to ask – but how do I know if this is a gem? Just knowing how to find a coin gives me nothing. And that is where real analysis steps in.

Doing Research

If you ever followed Cryptos on Twitter, you are probably aware of the famous question "What are your thoughts on <list any coin here>". In a way, it is very comfortable and easy to skip research while getting confirmation on whether the coin is worth investing in. However, the harsh truth, it will punish the person who asks more than it will help.

Research is individual and depends hugely on the person doing it – different values are appreciated and the trade time frame is not always the same, that is why it is hard to have two people having the same opinion on a coin. On top of that, doing your research brings something additional and almost as valuable as the knowledge about a currency itself – confidence in it. If you ever bought a coin without previously doing much checking on it, you probably know the feeling of urgency to sell when it is not moving for some time – that is the lack of research.

Understanding the potential value of the project is essential in holding and maximising gains. Without that knowledge, it is extremely easy to sell it before it has a chance to breakout (there is a joke circulating that the price jumps every time after you sell it, but there is more truth to it than humour).

Doing research requires a lot of time indeed, and it is a lot easier to ask your favourite influencer with a good track record what his thoughts are on the matter. The problem is that as long as that will remain the basis of your investing strategy, we can guarantee you will not be able to sustain your performance outside of ultra-bullish markets, where nobody loses.

But since you bought this book, we assume you wish to find out how to do it more efficiently, so without further ado, let's proceed to explain the research step by step.

To keep this as organised as possible, we have divided the research into two categories and will be talking about the specific parts of the research one by one.

Core Research
- Team
- Idea
- Development
- Coin Metrics

Additional Research
- Community
- Partnerships
- Advisors
- Token utility
- Distribution
- Competition
- Roadmap
- Presentation
- Market liquidity

Core Research

This segment describes the essential parts of any project – the issues listed in each category should raise concerns whether the investment is worth your money. This also means that further research is not necessary as the core fundamentals are not met with proper standards. Other additional categories are not valuable enough to cover up the shortcomings. Let's start with the most important one – the team.

Team

The team is what drives the project and is crucial to its success. You can have a lacklustre idea, weak coin metrics and no product, but with a strong team, there is a chance that in the end, the project will be as valuable as it was projected to be.

Same goes for the idea – even the best idea, with low coin supply and a working product, might not be sustained if the team is inexperienced or not diversified enough. Everything starts and ends with the people on the project – this should always be your first target of research.

What is essential when looking at the team? There are five points that, in our opinion, should be met to consider the squad being trustworthy:

Experience of team members

It does not only matter if the team worked for big companies like Microsoft or EY in the past. What matters is what kind of positions and responsibilities they previously held (are they suitable for their current position?) and how long did they work in there (a few years or a quick stint of few months that is less valuable?). Do not get blinded by those flashy company names – the experience there does not mean much if it does not fit with the current responsibilities a team member will have.

Experience in the industry

Take a close look if the members of the team have previous experience in that specific industry they are planning to work on now. It is not just an added advantage to know the market, but it is often a necessity because regulations and the overall stubbornness of industries require an excellent knowledge to innovate it. Do not expect bankers to succeed in social media or marketing experts to create the next investing tool if they have never traded Cryptocurrencies before.

Good diversity

Each team should have a core squad, and support cast around it that features people from different departments – marketing, finance, business development, developers, management, law advisors, community managers – the more varied a skillset of the team is, the better. For smaller coins, it is not, of course, a necessity as they work similarly to small start-ups (which they are). But when you have ICOs trying to raise 30/40/50 millions of dollars or projects already worth billions, you should expect the team to cover every part of business activity.

Entrepreneurial background

This applies to the core team (mostly, the CEO) and it is equally important. Try looking at the members as tools – even if they are the best tools on the market, you still need somebody to use them. Managing a project in the cryptosphere is a lot different than in regular markets – you are under constant pressure of community that demands quick results, very often under severe market conditions (try explaining the falling price of a coin during a bear market). The CEO needs to be a person that has worked in a tough environment before as the margin of error in crypto is tiny. Even breaking little promises, like not getting listed on new exchanges during the first few weeks after the ICO, might trigger a wave of FUD surrounding the project by ex-supporters that are disappointed with the execution, even if that was not the team's fault.

Development team

This is probably one of the most overlooked aspects of team research, which is a shame because it is crucial as well. Since blockchain is a very new technology and the project's idea revolves around it, it is important to have capable developers even if they are hard to come by. You will see dozens of ICO with powerful CEOs, marketing people who worked for Coca-Cola and probably other all-stars but absolutely zero developers and an empty Github. Without a team of people who will program the technology, nothing else the team can do really matters.

(While doing your research, make sure that if they do not have anybody on the team responsible for coding, they may have outsourced this process. If that is also not the case – the team's potential to deliver is insufficient and if they do – it probably means that blockchain was not needed in the first place anyway.)

Idea

The idea is the foundation of it all. It is the first thing that is being discussed when presenting the project and the impression made by it should be good enough to encourage the investor to go deeper into it. Similar to the team, there are a few standards that should be met to consider it investment-worthy:

Blockchain requirement

The biggest issue in all crypto-related projects right now is whether the idea needs a blockchain to work. Well – you do not need shoes to run – but it helps.

There is a fine line between a coin utilising blockchain because it is necessary and because it makes the company more efficient. In smart contract platforms, it is, but new projects often tend to use blockchain only to get into the cryptosphere (their primary focus is on raising money).

(Example of that might be Kryll – a simple trading platform automatizing trading strategies, where a very similar idea could have been realised without implementing blockchain technology (here used as a payment system for those strategies). Even the team admitted that one of the use cases of the token is to be able to raise money in the ICO.)

When thinking about a project, make sure that the usage of blockchain is justified – not only to serve as a payment method on the platform but also to solve problems with the coin. Otherwise, you are probably just facing a money grab, which we suggest staying away from.

(An excellent example of a proper blockchain application lies in the healthcare industry. The concept of sharing patient's data requires absolute privacy and security, which are blockchain's leading utilities. There are no other ways to replace those features, unlike trading platforms where having a token is an unnecessary luxury.)

Innovation

Since the whole market is about to disrupt every possible industry, the ideas that can be implemented in the blockchain sometimes feel futuristic (especially with the addition of artificial intelligence). Because of the growing popularity, the market is getting saturated in many of the industries. This requires new projects to appear with more innovative technology and older coins to keep up with the competition to be up to date. Cryptocurrencies are currently the fastest growing market out there, and coins that do not follow the speed of growth will become obsolete. Therefore, by looking at the idea make sure it has something to offer that no other project can. That is also the reason why some ICOs already work with Blockchain 4.0, while most of the people do not even know when 2.0 appeared.

(An example of that growth is evident on different platforms offering more and more TPS (transactions per second). Almost every few weeks we can see new ICOs promising 1 million TPS (Matrix AI, Credits) when Litecoin has 56 TPS, Ethereum 50 TPS and NEO 1000 TPS. So far, we are yet to see any blockchain fulfilling that promise.)

Easy to promote

As we talked about it earlier for a project to succeed it needs to be able to generate hype around it. That can be accomplished by either a significant development or an easy and comprehensive idea that can be caught up in the right place at the right time. Even if the technology is complex, the marketing of the concept should be as easy to understand as possible. This fits nicely with a saying around the community that many investors still cannot explain what blockchain is (this is often told as a joke, but the reality is not far away from it).

(Good example of that might be TomoChain, a project that utilises side-chains (which means nothing for an average investor) but is promoted as the coin that solves Ethereum's scalability issues (a widespread problem yet to be resolved).)

High technology can get lost in the crowd if it is not promoted correctly. The most important approaches should be directed towards the investors and not geeks who understand the technology. So, even if the coin on your radar is highly technical, make sure it has plans on how to attract the public to it.

Possible to implement

Another significant issue that is often overlooked is the ability to implement the ideas listed in roadmaps. It is an issue of a long-term investment as the current price is influenced by current events and does not consider the far future. If you are planning to invest in the project, you should pick the one that is ambitious, but still achievable.

It is a mixture of all the other elements (team, partnerships, competition etc.) that allows the project to achieve its goals, but if they are flawed from the structural perspective, it makes little sense to trust it.

(An example of that might be Nucleus Vision, which works with sensors that can track motion and mobile IDs. The idea works well in the early stages but looking further into their plans reveals some issues. Those devices are supposed to be used in large venues (when the coverage is roughly 200M) to help catch known criminals and to prevent threats (when none of the current functions can even remotely come close to achieving this). Nobody says that it will not evolve in the

future, but as of right now, in early development stages, plans like these are pure speculation and should not be the basis for a long-term investment.)

Development

We have talked about how hype can often outperform working products, but we should at least expect a company to have developed something in place. This should be one of the priorities when thinking about investing in an ICO, and it is a significant advantage for any coin already on the market. Along with the cryptosphere maturing, the projects that show development will be the ones that will be more appreciated than the ones built on empty promises (valued solely on speculation). The two points to check are:

MVP

Not many projects in crypto can show real results yet, which might sound confusing considering that it is a hundred-billion-dollar industry, but that is the nature of emerging markets. Having a product ready to show puts the coin above probably 95% of the overall competition, but that does not mean it is yet worth the higher positions on CoinMarketCap. The valuation of the product should be conducted like in any other market:

- At what stage it is (alpha, beta, full release?) and how is the user's experience?

- How many people already use it (if it is an app, how many people downloaded it?)

- What are the reviews, are there any bugs?

- Is it used by people outside of Crypto as well?

Any question that gives you a bright idea of how successful the current state of the product is. There are no golden rules here, however, in the case of applications and social media projects, in general, make sure to check if the data provided by the company is not fake. *(For example, the number of active users, which is often counted from the climax while the app itself is dead 90% of the time).*

As an investor, you are looking for coins with a working product and an undervalued low market cap, but sometimes investing in projects with less development is not a bad idea either. If the coin has upcoming major releases, it might very often bring more profits to the table than the already established currency, since it will generate more noise. If you look in the long-term perspective, the safer bet will always be the one with working technology waiting to expand. But as a trader, do not be afraid to look for coins that are in the middle of significant developments, as those hype waves are usually the best opportunities currently available on the market.

Proof of work

In theory, every project that tries to raise money should have something to show, but as you will find out while going through different ICOs, that is often not the case. If the product is yet to be released, it is essential to have some proof of actual work being done in the project. That can take the shape of an available code on GitHub or an alpha/beta version of the product. The important thing is that there is steady progress being done towards the release.

Most of the projects indeed have a public GitHub to track the code being released by the team; therefore, this should be one of the first places to check while doing your research. Make sure that the commits in there are being regularly updated (the vast majority of ICOs do it once and then do not check their GitHub for weeks) and if they do not – contact the team members to ask why the repository is not active. Depending on the project, you will either hear that they are keeping it private, and it should be released soon, or a brief message "will get back to you" from the admin which should start raising some concerns since they rarely come back.

Apart from the code itself, there must also be progress in the business as well, such as partnerships being signed, new team member additions, attending meetings, conferences. Every sign of activity is essential and might be a clue of the direction the project is taking – the more of it, the better. A simple communication about "work being done" in the background of a social channel is not sufficient. If the work is done, there must be some proof of it, otherwise empty promises and declarations might very quickly turn the community against the coin, from which it rarely recovers.

Coin Metrics

Since we are talking about investing, it is evident that we want the highest ROI (Return On Investment) as soon as possible. In Cryptocurrencies, the price is not the only thing that matters – most of the time, it is very misleading; therefore, an investor should be aware of all the other existing metrics like circulating/total supply or market cap.

Even the fundamentally best projects might not be worth an investment because the chances of growth are simply non-existent due to unfavourable metrics (since the price in crypto is very volatile and follows market cycles frequently, purchases based only on fundamentals are often a recipe for disaster). Once you get to know what the project is about, these are the points you should check next to decide if the risk/return ratio is favourable:

Market Cap

The market cap is a simple equation - circulating supply * price. It is the total valuation of the project and should be the first thing to look at when doing your research. It is the market cap that defines whether a plan is undervalued or not, therefore comparing coins to its competitors should also be done accordingly to this metric. Be aware that it might experience some rapid changes not only because of the price change but also because of a potential coin release from the team, which is directly being priced into the total capitalisation of the project.

(Sometimes ICOs keep the coins of investors locked-up for some time, before releasing them. The additional supply automatically increases market cap than often is rebalanced by decreasing price.)

What can be considered as a low/mid/high cap, very much depends on the current stage of the market. Microcap once defined a coin below 250K, and now it might be below 1M. Same goes for high caps as even in early 2017 being worth over a billion was considered massive, while in April 2018 already top 25 coins qualify into that group, with a lot more looming to join once the total capitalisation goes up again.

As you might guess, lower market cap equals higher returns, but also higher risks. The lower a market cap is, the smaller the liquidity and higher the possibility of manipulating the market by big players, therefore they should be approached with caution. Depending on your style of play and strategy, betting on right coins with smaller market caps might be hugely profitable, especially if the fundamentals point at them having a chance of becoming one of the top 50 projects in Cryptocurrencies.

Price

Probably the most misunderstood metric in the whole crypto is the price, as it is still a point of debate how important the low price of the token is. Before we answer that, we need to address one crucial thing – low dollar value does not mean a coin is cheap and high dollar value does not mean a coin is expensive. Price is strictly correlated with market cap; therefore, a coin worth 1 cent with 10 billion in supply (100 million dollars in market cap) is a lot more expensive than a coin worth 1 dollar with 1000 in supply (1000 dollars in market cap). The real value of the project is seen in market cap, as it is an indicator of how much money was invested in a particular asset. The goal is to buy those coins that show more potential returns, so those that are yet to experience a massive inflow of money. A single unit price is in no way an indicator of that value.

That does not mean, however, that low coin price does not have its advantages because it does – it is a psychological perk that makes buying a massive number of cheap tokens a lot more satisfying than only a few of a big price. Not only that, we would go as far as saying that the majority of people who are not into crypto have no idea how to evaluate a project; therefore, they are looking solely at a price as an indicator. That makes coins like Verge, Cardano or Kin extremely undervalued in their eyes. Knowing this provides an excellent trading opportunity as you are playing into the masses mindset, which could prove very profitable if the coin gets more attention, especially with the so-called "dumb money" that is unfamiliar with market cap.

Supply

Knowing how the market cap and the price work, there is not much to say about the supply besides one difference between the circulating supply and total supply. Circulating supply is the one that counts into the market cap and represents the number of coins currently available for trading (in other words – not locked up, as they can be moved from wallets onto the exchanges).

The second type – total supply – is the maximum amount of coins that can exist for a specific project. The difference between the total supply and the circulating supply represents the coins not available. The reason for them being locked up might be because they are not mined yet (for PoW coins) or because they are locked up by the ICO for a specified period, waiting to be released. The focus should be on the circulating supply as that is the current representation of the situation but be aware of the total as well in case the difference is too big (everything from double and up should raise questions and be further investigated - besides PoW). If the disparity is too big, make sure to understand the reason – you never want to be in a situation where unreleased tokens could crash the market any second or that the regular releases of big amounts would deploy too much supply for the existing demand that would stop value appreciation.

The smaller the supply, the better, as it gives more room for growth to early investors and that is what we are looking for in a quality long-term hold.

Additional Research

This category should confirm your bullish sentiment towards a particular project. Going through all those additional categories probably won't change your decision on investing but can boost your confidence in it, especially if you are planning it to be a long-term play.

Community

The only reason why the community is not in the Core Research section is that the coin needs good fundamentals in the first place to gather people around it. Having a passionate group of supporters does wonders to the project, as it equips it with the most effective form of marketing out there – word-of-mouth. Strong community makes any update on progress a lot more visible and is essential if the coin wants to see steady growth, instead of a quick pump & dump due to people being interested only during a specific event.

To research the strength of the community, you should visit all the coin's channels and find out how many members are out there and what the activity level is (very often huge ICO groups with hundreds of thousands of followers are less active than 300 people community of a low cap). Check what are the topics they bring up – are the conversations about development and support for the coin or is the channel spammed with overinvested people looking for quick news and new exchange listings? The quality of the discussion is an excellent indicator on what to expect – the supportive community will provide help and spread the good news, while bagholders will interrupt the regular work of the team (or community managers). This will not only reject new investors wanting to get to know the project but will ruin the team's chances of gathering positive feedback from the healthy part of the community.

(Probably the most popular community out there is the one of Verge, as it reached legendary status in the cryptosphere. People supporting Verge were so committed to helping the coin succeed, they even raised 3 million dollars among themselves for the purpose of Verge signing a secret partnership that required the money to finalise the deal. Later it turned out that the collaboration was with Pornhub, which now (April 2018) accepts Verge as the payment on their site.)

Partnerships

Every project in Cryptoworld is basically a start-up; therefore, it should be evaluated as a business. Merely developing a product will not mean a thing, if there is nobody out there to use it. A lot of people like to invest in those PoW coins that have hard-working developers and were started from scratch and not due to fundraising. The problem is that the majority of these coins have absolutely no utility and if 2017/2018 surge of ICOs showed anything, it is that business-oriented projects are taking over the spotlight. Cryptocurrencies are not being solely evaluated on their tech-side like TPS (transactions per second) anymore – business adoption matters as well.

While looking at the partnerships, you need to see the value that the company can bring to the table. There are dozens of ICOs coming out that are partnered with other crypto-related projects, but the problem is that often neither of those parties have anything to show yet. Having a partnership with a company that will not be able to use your product or present you theirs, has currently only speculation purposes. The real value comes from cooperation that links the project to the regular markets and real organisations.

(Example of a collaboration like this is Request Network working together on a payment system with PwC France. This not only creates an excellent opportunity for REQ but also validates its long-term position in the cryptosphere, where many other projects will probably disappear due to the lack of real business utility.)

(Outside of that there are of course positive crypto-to-crypto partnerships as well. Example of that might be Hacken or Quantstamp, both of which do auditing of the smart contracts for different projects, mostly ICOs. It is an effective cooperation that brings results instantly and does not act only as a speculation tool.)

Always look for projects that aim to get partnerships done. It shows their understanding of how to run a real business and not another forked gambling coin. Also, while researching partnerships, always make sure to have a proof they indeed exist. More on how to do that can be found shortly after this section in the "Red Flags" segment.

Advisors

Advisors are very often put into the same bracket as the team members, but that should not be the case. Advisors will not develop the product nor will they sign new partnerships. Their role is often overrated because usually, those people have a very rich background which is so easy to pick up (blockchain expert from Ethereum or managers from Microsoft/Goldman Sachs). Even the best set of advisors will not make up for a lacklustre team as their role is often highly unspecified and very rarely there are signs of their frequent activity within the project. It does not mean, however, that they do not bring any value.

When looking at advisors you should first check the position and industry that they come from – can they help in any way with their experience? Even if they are not heavily involved in the project, they still provide valuable business contacts and insights that might help the team. Next, try to evaluate their potential level of activity – are those the people who advice 10 ICOs at the same time or maybe is it a person that treats that position as a regular job (per LinkedIn information)? Finally – look for a potential hype catalyst. As I mentioned before, advisors are often used by shills to show the power of the team/project, so the presence of a big name could potentially ease the way to more exposure.

(An ICO called Current had in its advisory board Mark Cuban – a serial entrepreneur, one of the biggest names circulating in the cryptosphere. This alone was one of the most significant selling points for the ICO, even though he never actually spoke about the company in public.)

Token utility

Not many people talk about how crucial token utility is because it usually requires more in-depth research to find out where the token is going to be used.

Even with the best team and partnerships around, in theory, a token should not increase in value if it has no utility inside of the project. However, since we know that the price is not always the rational reflection of the fundamentals, coins tend to pump even with terrible or no token utility at all. That happens in the name of "token is the representation of the company".

(Example of a bad utility is Dotcoin from Cryptopia exchange. Its main purpose is to be a currency that must be bought if a new project wants to get listed on the platform. The problem is that it offers nothing besides that and the original utility could have been swapped with any other currency out there, and it would not change a thing. However, that does not stop the coin from making

500%/1000% gains once every few months during alt season.)

Even if the use case of the coin is often ignored, it doesn't change the fact that well-thought utility is a big advantage to the project. While doing your research, look at what kind of use cases for the coin the team is trying to provide. Is the coin just a simple "fuel" - a payment method - on the platform that is developed or does it have a real value that cannot be subbed by any other currency? This aspect may not matter very much in the early stages of the development, but once the product is running, all eyes are focused on how the coin works within the company.

(One of the better use cases for the token can be seen in Restart Energy MWAT project, which was mentioned before as an energy coin. On this platform, tokens are backed by real energy that can be used by individuals in their households. That is, on top of being a cornerstone of the platform's franchise model and overall payment method. It is one of those rare cases where the token actually cannot be swapped by any other currency, while still maintaining platform's functions.)

Distribution

Fair distribution of coins is vital for the steady growth of their value. With only a few addresses holding the majority of the supply, there is always a risk of the owner manipulating the price. The more balanced the distribution is, the lower the chances are of anybody having real control over the price. It is also hard to say what is a good score since every team controls a different amount of coins, but be careful with any project having top 100 addresses holding more than 90% of the coins (especially in few big chunks that do not belong to the team).

To check how the division of coins looks like, among all the existing contracts, you can use the Token Holders tab on https://etherscan.io/ after you select the currency of your interest. Most of the time there will be one prominent address holding 20% or more of overall supply – that is usually the team, so it is not a reason to be concerned but make sure that this information was provided earlier.

Competition

Having a bunch of coins in the same area is excellent for the whole market as it keeps it more competitive. It is also very favourable for individual currencies, as very often projects that are directly in competition tend to pump closely to each other.

(Recently (April 2018) that could have been seen with Wanchain and Fusion (direct competitors, cross-chain platforms) or with IOTA and its Internet-of-things competitors like ITC which jumped shortly after IOTA finished its crazy run from 80 cents to over 5 dollars.)

Since most projects in the cryptosphere are still not even close to having a prototype, the fact that two coins are aiming to do the same thing adds even more speculation to an already hype-driven market. You should understand that the superior project is not always going to come out on top, especially if it launched later. As legendary economist John Keynes once said - Markets can remain irrational for longer than you can remain solvent.

When looking at the competition from the core fundamentals perspective, you should do standard research (using this chapter as a guide) and see if any elements differ positively. If there is no significant advantage over projects being higher, do not expect to match them just because the technology is the same. With so many coins currently on the market, no mediocrity will be allowed to pump significantly, if there are no reasons for it outside of competition having a higher cap. Those pumps occur because people are looking for higher returns on investment (from cheaper coins) but there is a limit on how high a project can go based solely on the comparison.

If the coin you are looking at does have advantages over its competitors, see the difference in market caps and judge if it is possible to catch up to the competitor based on the significance of the disparity between those projects. If it is – that is a good target and possibly an auspicious opportunity since it is easier to build exposure based on a comparison to the project that already has a significant audience.

To summarise - fundamentals in the case of competition are highly dependent on the disparity between the projects. The closer they are to each other, the more important the fundamentals are. Same thing the other way – if the difference is significant, trying to catch a project with a higher cap will possibly be profitable, but because of an established position and usually bigger community, sudden change of places should not be expected.

Roadmap

A roadmap allows you to see if the project has a well-thought long-term plan for itself. On this basis, we can evaluate what time frame we should take the trade and if there is potential for the future. Some things to look at while rating the roadmap:

- Complexity – how detailed is the description of specific goals? Is it just "Beta launch" or are the functions described as well? Level of complexity shows that the development is well-thought and planned, providing more confidence in the team delivering what they promised (instead of missing out on parts of development due to delays etc.)

- Diversity – what is the roadmap focusing on? Mostly on the development or does it expand to other markets/exchange listings? The more comprehensive the overview of different business categories is, the better since it shows you that the team understands the need not only to develop a product but to promote it as well.

- Attainability – are the goals possible to achieve? If there are any numbers – are they backed by any specific calculations? Being ambitious is good, but targets should also be rational. Watch out for the projects which promise big exchanges in their roadmap when it is often not their decision if they will get listed. Also, if there are any predictions on the number of users and future revenue – make sure those are backed by some real data and not just by blind guesses.

- Length – how long is the roadmap? Does it have plans for the next year or the next couple of years? A long-term vision is always better but be aware of the projects that do not have their product launched in the shorter period (or at least alpha/beta of it). There should be reasons for people to talk about the coin at every stage of the development to make it a worthwhile investment.

- Precision – how precise are they with the timeline? Are they aiming at Q1/Q2 or is the roadmap divided by months? The more accurate it is, the bigger the pressure is on the team to deliver since they are giving themselves a tiny margin of error.

Lack of the roadmap is not that rare, especially with smaller coins, since they focus more on the development and update their progress along the way. For projects with a higher cap, however, having a roadmap became a standard. This provides greater transparency for the coin's future, and it should be expected.

Presentation

As we already mentioned before, projects that are easy to sell are the ones that usually pump the hardest. From this point of view, it is crucial for the coin to have a good branding and overall presentation. Everything here counts – logo, name, ticker – as that is what stays with the buyers and helps to spread the coin further through the community.

(Very often coins go through a rebranding to be more appealing. One of the best examples was NEO which rebranded from AntShares, going from 5/6 dollars to a spectacular 47 dollars in a matter of a month near the time of rebranding.)

When evaluating a coin, make sure it has no flaws in the first impression that might make it hard for first-time investors to remember the coin. There are no real rules besides an overall good feeling of the brand, but it should be reasonably easy to see any shortcomings.

(Rock token has a ticker of $RKT, which is very often a target for jokes pointing at how close it is to #REKT. This could be a success as it gives more attention, but we have also seen people stay away from investing because of the poor choice of letters.)

Apart from branding, it is essential to visit the website and make sure it is updated and prepared professionally. Some points you should take into consideration while doing your research are:

- Is the site clear/easy to navigate through?
- Are there any spelling mistakes, bad graphics used?
- Are the selling points of the coin highlighted?
- Is the language of the White Paper/website concrete and technical or is it a word salad (more on this later in this chapter)?
- If the team is not anonymous, is it presented and described with LinkedIn links to it?

Generally, we would suggest not to place much emphasis on the website itself comparing to other aspects of the projects (development, team etc.), but it certainly helps if the site is done professionally and does not deter potential investors.

Market Liquidity

Market liquidity should matter most for day-traders, but investors will also need to know about it when planning an entry. Market liquidity describes how easy it would be for you to buy in or cash out, depending on the number of coins that you own. The more exchanges listed a coin, the better, as it increases the volume - it is never wise to depend only on one platform (as it can block trading due to maintenance period etc.).

The issue of the lack of liquidity is mostly relevant for lower caps. It brings many risks to the investor; therefore, you should always be wary of what you are getting into and evaluate if it is worth entering the trade at this exact moment. The risks include:

-   Inability to cash out of your investment due to the lack of buying pressure (leaving you basically frozen with your coins)

-   The possibility of a market crash (because of thin order books it is very easy for even one person to crash the price almost to zero at any given moment)

-   Risk of the coin being delisted due to lack of volume. A lot of exchanges remove coins that are unable to generate volume which automatically results in a big crash, that for micro caps with no exposure is extremely hard to recover from.

Buying such coins, however, also has some perks to it, since it is usually the lowest point you could invest in a project if you consider it valuable from FA perspective. The more exchanges (of high quality) a project is listed on, the bigger the chances of the exponential growth are, but similar results can be obtained with hitting a right low cap, yet to be listed on any significant platform.

Difference between regular and ICO research

Since we got a regular research behind us, it is important to mention the differences between researching coins already on the market and ICOs.

More pressure on development

Having a working product should be an extremely important factor for any trader that wants to see a quick return on their investment. This happens because:

- ICO, compared to the coins already on the market, has yet to prove that is has any value. You simply should not give money away for a pack of promises as there is no guarantee they will ever be fulfilled. With coins on the market the risk is a lot smaller as they need to deliver to stay on it.

- A good ICO usually gets a lot of publicity that raises the awareness around the whole community. Therefore, as it starts being a recognizable project, it needs to show proof that a strong development is actually taking place. A popular ICO cannot rely on gaining value thanks to the hype alone.

- It minimizes the risks of the project being a scam. That is only one of the many ways of confirming the legitimacy of the ICO, but nonetheless – it is an important proof.

More pressure on red flags

Since ICOs are still largely unregulated and the Cryptoworld is full of unexperienced investors, a lot of scammers are trying to take advantage of that. At least few times a month there are reports of another ICO running away with investor's money - usually without any consequences.

(In many cases that could have been avoided as many of those projects give blatant signals – recently there was an ICO in which actor Ryan Gosling was listed as one of the team members. It is often happening during a bull market when ICOs have no problems raising 30 million dollars or more, since people are a lot less picky with their next investments. A thorough analysis of all the project's aspects is compulsory before investing into a crowd sale to minimize the risk of it being a scam.)

A list of the important points to take into consideration while evaluating a project's legitimacy is available at the end of this small chapter.

ICO metrics

ICO metrics are basically the equivalent to coin metrics when doing a regular research. While you also have to check the price of the token and the supply, with ICOs you also need to take a look at the fundraising hard cap and token distribution.

To estimate if a certain price is low, you should look at the supply. What matters here is the ratio between these two, although as we mentioned earlier, it bears repeating, the lower the price in dollar value, the more appealing it might look to others.

(Let's say an average price is 1$ with 100M coins in supply. If that is our golden standard (it is the one we would recommend) then 1B supply should have a price of 0.10$, 10B supply a price of 0.01$ and so on. Everything above that ratio (for example 0.50$ with 1B supply is extremely high) points at lower ROI.)

Maybe even more important is the hard cap of the ICO that decides what the limit of supply is going to be. General rule – the lower the cap the better, since not a lot of people will be able to buy coins, which creates a high demand once it is listed on exchanges. Same goes the other way – if the hard cap is high (in March 2018 we would define 25M as the average cap) it usually fills the demand, which lowers the remaining demand.

We would highly suggest staying away from the ICOs with high caps (and even worse – ICOs with no cap at all) even if the fundamentals are strong, with the sole reason of a possible better entry once they hit the exchanges. While evaluating this, take a closer look at the lock-up period as that might be a way for the ICO to create more demand before it gets listed (more on this later).

It is also important to understand what the terms in private and public sales are. Usually, both the price and bonuses are a lot better during the private sale that is why it is a lot harder to get in it - typically it rewards the biggest investors. If the difference of those two is significant (half the token price with significant part of the hard cap available, for example) be careful, because that often gives early investors the ability to manipulate the market at the beginning. The same is valid for bonuses – huge number of additional tokens for early participants (basically anything above 40%) is troubling.

Finally, check how the tokens are distributed in the ICO. Since the team gathers a lot of money during the fundraising, it is not a good feature if they still plan to keep a large amount of the supply for themselves (anything above 40% for the team/advisors and other developments should raise some concerns). No matter what the distribution rate is, you should also always find out how the locked-up tokens are going to be used – the team should be transparent on how are they are planning on spending them, a simple "project development" is not sufficient. If the distribution plan is logical and the ICO requires having a bigger number of tokens saved for later, do not count low allocation for investors as a red flag. It is important to be flexible at all times.

All this information must be public for all the ICO participants and if it is not, make sure the team provides it. Otherwise it should raise a lot of questions among the community (possibility of hiding better terms for private investors).

Duration of a lock-up

A lock-up period is the time between participating in the ICO and receiving the tokens, which are held by the team.

Each ICO has a different model when it comes to the time frame of the token release. Some do it directly after the crowd sale on decentralized exchanges (or with an already established one) while others have the tokens locked-up for weeks or months until they get listed on a bigger platform. The importance of this time frame lies within the market conditions as that is often a crucial factor for the token's price upon the listing.

Quicker listings work well in a bull market where investors are looking for a quick return on their investment, therefore most quality ICOs open 2/3x over the initial value even a few days after the crowd sale is done. In a bear market, on the other hand, it is basically an instant loss as there is very little demand in the market, unless the project had a very low hard cap that might counter low demand with even a lower supply.

Longer lock-ups very much depend on the state of the market. Usually, in bullish conditions a delayed listing helps the token to increase in value as the team continuously delivers news and new developments increase the hype for those that missed out. After an extremely long lock-up, Wanchain started at around 10x of its initial ICO price even if market conditions were not favourable.

The lock-up period has its downside as the wrong timing (buy in bull market, release the token in a bear one) could not only lead to a decrease in value, but also has an opportunity cost to it (meaning that other trades could have been processed with that money during this period). It is rare that a coin released after a few months of a bull market does not get listed above its initial price but the most common period varies from 2 weeks to a month. In that time frame, make sure that the market conditions are stable, because otherwise, depending on the quality of the ICO, the risk/reward ratio is usually not favourable.

Hype

As we mentioned the hype's role in short-term investments before, the same applies to ICOs as well. Getting more recognition is essential to getting the crowd sale sold out and making people feel like they missed out on the opportunity. The main goal for the investor is to get into the crowd sale that not only has a high demand, but also a limited supply. If those 2 requirements are met, it probably means that buying the ICO itself will not be an easy task - usually it involves a whitelist getting closed very quickly and the ICO being sold out in the first couple minutes, often leaving whitelisted investors without their tokens. We suggest registering on multiple interesting crowd sales even before doing research on them (that requires only e-mail address in most cases) as the list might be unavailable the next time we hear of them. Registering for a crowd sale that does mean you have to participate in it.

In case there is not enough buying pressure, there are no reasons for investing in the ICO as the coins can be easily grabbed after the listing, usually at the lower price.

More pressure on the presentation

Since ICOs need to lure investors into their proposition, the first impression is crucial. The website should be clear and easy to understand. The presentation of the team should be complex and the website should include all the necessary elements – ICO metrics, roadmap, FAQ, media coverage etc. The White Paper should be concrete and focus on business aspects of the project such as marketing plans, development timeline and market analysis. Stay away from papers that look like a word salad with a lot of plans and promises but no substance or proof that the ideas can be accomplished.

In presentation, we also include the way the team communicates during the ICO. Is the team constantly available to answer questions and if they do – are they successful? A well-organized telegram group without spamming is a very rare occurrence in today's ICO landscape and speaks volumes about the team's professionalism. It is important to see if they interact with their investors on various platforms (Twitter, YouTube, Reddit) and if they react to comments (ICO Bench, mentions on social channels). The lack of commitment at the beginning of the road not only hinders their own chances of getting the ICO sold out, but also fails to build a community which is essential for further growth.

Remember to also keep a close look on how the communication changes after the crowd sale is done. Majority of the ICOs suddenly stop uploading videos on YouTube and tend to be less active on social channels as the marketing is not necessary anymore. Try finding a team that will continue their hard work in a form of regular updates on the progress while keeping good contact with the community across social media channels.

Red flags/scams

It is not a secret that in a market with no regulations like crypto, scams are of daily occurrence. Not only dozens of PoW coins are launched every single day, there are also a lot of recent scam ICOs, which ran away with huge amounts of money. The style in which they do it is very different - Prodeum ICO closed all their channels and only left the website with "penis" written at the top left corner, while Bitcoiin ICO used Steven Seagal as an ambassador just to officially announce management leaving the project shortly after raising the money. In most of these cases, the shadiness was pretty easy to spot but as we already mentioned before, people do not do their research properly, therefore a lot of them are still tricked by scams. To always be sure you are dealing with a legit project, make sure to do a check-list of following points:

Team authenticity

This should be the priority during any research – never stop by simply going through information listed on the website. Make sure every team member has connections with the company (usually through LinkedIn) and that any advisor is also on the board. When there is no direct link from the website to confirm the team members and their experience it should not instantly raise concerns. However, if within a further research you are still having a hard time to affirm that those people are working for the company – we highly suggest staying away from that investment. There is no single reason why an ICO or an aspiring new coin would hide away information about their public team.

This, of course, does not apply to many small PoW coins where the team wants to remain anonymous – in that case, make sure to talk to them on one of the social media channels (Discord or Telegram most likely) to sense how genuine they are and how serious their approach to the project is. Investing in teams like this is obviously riskier as there are no consequences for them to exit scamming, but that is also the nature of the cryptosphere that cannot really be altered.

Company information

Another very important aspect of the research is making sure that the company has legal ground behind it (in other words – make sure it is a legit company, that is registered, has its office etc). That information should be visible at the bottom of the website or by googling it. If that does not appear, make sure to ask the team members on their social media channels for it. The response should also tell you a lot – if the team is delaying giving you the details or simply bans you from the channel that should immediately raise red flags as the lack of official company data makes it extremely easy for the ICO to run away with the money without any consequences.

This does not apply to smaller coins with anonymous team as that is the nature of the coin – that is how decentralized projects work so it would be irrational to expect real company information from a coin that consists of few programmers living around the globe and communicating with each other through Discord.

Large premine

A significant premine (anything outside of few % basically) is always a big concern, same as uneven distribution. Putting a big amount of supply in the hands of one person/team, especially on smaller PoW coins is a big risk. Always look for the explanation of the premine and be suspicious of larger amounts being held, as that is usually not necessary to continue with the development of the coin and no project should be trusted fully.

No code repository

Lack of Github (a website where teams upload their code) or basically any other proof of work should always be considered a huge red flag. Unless there is a reason from the team on why they do not want to disclose their development (as they are afraid of somebody stealing the work as an example), there is absolutely no reason why investors should not be able to have a clear view on the current state of the project.

Buzz word salad

This one is very subjective and points more towards level of quality than being a scam, but it is still worth noting. Very often the websites and ICOs are filled with hype words in the kind of "revolutionary", "next generation", "superior" etc. which make a very good impression on non-experienced investors but in fact, have little to no value.

The trick is to be able to communicate even the more complicated idea in a language that is both understandable and specific so that it shows the expertise of a team. Not being able to talk about the technical nature of the project may raise some concerns especially if there is no demo or product yet to see, as there are many coins which offer nothing besides good marketing (there are ICOs coming out every day that try to raise 30 million dollars based solely on their White Paper). Another famous crypto saying is "Scams pump the hardest". You should be aware that if a legit project is using this kind of language there is high chance that it will get picked up by the community as it is "catchy". If it does, make sure that they also have something technical to show.

Plagiarism

Plagiarism is not the worst sin a project could commit, but it is a reason to worry if it does happen. It concerns mostly White Papers and recently a lot of ICOs were caught copying (such as DADI). The significance of that depends largely on how the company explains itself. The explanation says a lot about the coin and its management – the team being able to apologize for the plagiarism, might even bring more good than bad to the whole situation, but that is very rarely the case. Usually companies are trying to explain themselves with the likes of using the same sources as the other White Paper, which just continues to reject potential investors from it because of the lack of honesty. There are individual cases as well, like companies already in existence having problems with adjusting to crypto standards (as White Paper is treated like a business plan and they have little knowledge about it), but it still does not mitigate the effects of copying someone else's work.

Plagiarizing a White Paper shows a high level of either laziness or incompetence and should never be accepted. Sometimes, however, the significance of this action can be downgraded if there are no other reasons to doubt the project and the reaction from the company was satisfying. After all, the only thing that matters is the delivery of the product, therefore do not try to reject the project instantly under those accusations as in the future these bloopers might turn out to be non-events.

Celebrity Endorsement

This is not as big as fake team members or lack of code but if the history tells us something, it is that ICOs promoted by big names (Paris Hilton, Steven Seagal, DJ Khaled) very often turn out to be either scams or just terrible investments. If a project cannot promote itself in other ways than hiring celebrities with absolutely no connection to Cryptocurrencies, you should probably stay away from investing in it. Best projects focus on development and delivering the product, not on getting cheap recognition from the public that is probably not even aware of what an ICO is.

Fake partnerships

This is one of the most common ways scam projects are trying to create hype around them. Faking partnerships can have a few different forms:

- Showcasing a partnership as a sealed deal even if it is still in talking phase. This was the case with few Chinese projects that were later removing "partners" logos from their website since the deal never went through. Not very common, but there are cases of sudden partnerships disappearing from ICOs sites right after the sale is closed.

- Exaggerating the significance of the partnership. Two examples from real crypto life - using BMW's data base which is open for every third-party project does not mean a company is partnered with BMW. Same way having a partnership with a shop that sells Tommy Hilfiger clothes in it does not mean that the company is partnered with the Tommy Hilfiger brand. This is one of the most popular ways of misleading investors and it is often met with non-scam companies as well. Very few teams actually showcase any documents proving they have a deal in place which is a shame as that would greatly benefit the community surrounding the project.

- Straight out lying about having a partnership done. This is done by basically only blatant scams with a bunch of other red flags all around it, but it is still common.

In order to check it, simply contact the team directly or try searching for a proof online/at the source (potential partner). Since the awareness for scams is growing month by month there is a high chance that this kind of research was already done by Twitter, therefore make sure that the answer is not flowing somewhere already to avoid creating unnecessary FUD.

The last note on exposing scams: being listed on a huge exchange does not always mean the project is completely legit. Of course, the restrictions of getting listed on Binance or Bittrex are high so that the danger of investing in a scam is limited to almost zero, but there are cases like Centra which was charged by SEC which led to being delisted from Binance. With a market as young as Cryptocurrencies, no project should be taken for granted and any kind of suspicion should be taken seriously into consideration, as often the value dropping to zero can be quicker than your login into the exchange.

Market sentiment

If there was one tool that is as successful in predicting price bottoms and tops as Technical Analysis is, it would definitely be the market sentiment. From the next chapters, you will be able to see that there are certain emotions connected to the typical price cycle of a coin and that it often allows traders to evaluate if the peak of the growth is close. Another very popular trading rule – "Buy the fear, sell the greed" - the bottom is usually near when people start capitulating from their investments while accusing projects of being scams (without any particular evidence).

(This could've been seen during 2018 downtrend when Bitcoin was hovering around 6800$ mark as clear majority of traders predicted targets ranging from 5000$ to even 1000$. To the surprise of many not long after that Bitcoin jumped to over 9000$ leaving all people shorting underwater. The other side of the deal works exactly the same – once a coin is getting called the next Bitcoin and people brag about how much money they made from it, it is usually a signal that it is time to sell (Just like the old Wall Street saying states "When your cab driver starts talking about an asset, it is time to sell"). One of the best examples for that is Ethereum, where the last two tops where both met with people cheering for "The Flippening" which means that it would swap places with Bitcoin as the most valuable currency. At the time, Twitter was going absolutely wild with its lofty targets, only to be quickly brought down to earth with a multi-week downtrend that followed after that parabolic growth.)

The market never allows the majority to win that is why it is important to countertrade the overall sentiment when it is getting either euphoric or close to capitulation. We will be talking more on this in the Investment Strategies chapter, but before we do that – let's have a quick lesson on Technical Analysis.

Technical Analysis

A brief explanation before we begin this chapter – this section is not supposed to teach you every nuance of Technical Analysis. Learning TA is a long process that basically never ends as there is always something new to discover. The best teacher here is the experience which can only be gained by spending hours and hours in front of the charts, drawing them by yourself. What we want to accomplish with this chapter is to help you read any chart you will see going forward, as well as give you the basics to start creating your own. Our explanation of specific tools will consist of the brief definition and their use cases shown on the Cryptocurrency examples. If you want to study any of them in more detail, we will be listing valuable sources at the end of this book.

Role of Technical Analysis in crypto investing

Firstly, you should understand that TA does not provide clear predictions on the price. It serves as the analysis of the previous action and only predicts potential outcomes. It should never be taken for granted, especially in the crypto market which is easily manipulated.

There is a lot of discussion on whether TA actually works and if it does if it is more reliable than FA. We experienced enough to know that it does work but we stand in the middle of that conflict. We believe that TA and FA can and should be matched – you decide on what to invest in by the fundamentals, but you enter based on the chart. Lacking any of those two either limits your understanding of the potential or exposes you to a bad entry. With liquidity in many markets being so low, no chart can predict the next price spike due to a famous person tweeting about it. Having a complete image is the way to go in the cryptosphere if you really want to take advantage of what this market is offering.

You should also understand that there is not one right way of doing TA. Everybody has their own methods, as there is no right or wrong here. As long as you are successful in your setups, no tools that you will be using can be considered wrong. Try looking up to other traders to see how they are doing their analysis but always seek to find what works best for you.

TA basics

Before we start going through all the indicators, we need to present three basic concepts of TA by John J. Murphy, that are the foundation of the methodology:

The market discounts everything

This is the main argument of the people claiming that trading can be done solely with TA without the knowledge of fundamentals. The concept here is that every news/announcement/rumour is already priced into the chart. The price action is the reflection of every fundamental factor that affects the coin. In theory, this would mean that there is no need to follow the project's development if the effects of it will be visible on the chart anyway. However, the understanding of the fundamentals allows the investor to evaluate if the price appreciation was already strong enough or if it will continue leading to the event.

Price moves in trends

No matter which time frame we are looking at, the price always follows a trend (uptrend or downtrend). That price has a higher chance of continuing going with the current trend than to experience a reversal. It is a job of the analyst to recognise the trend as early as possible so that they can take advantage of it. Those trends can differ from each other depending on the time frame – price can be in a short-term downtrend while still being in a long-term uptrend (a small correction before continuation).

Between the trends, price often experiences so-called consolidation zones – those are the periods where the price is neither in an uptrend or downtrend but moves sideways before deciding its further direction. We will be using this term a lot later in this chapter; therefore, we would like to explain it now.

History tends to repeat itself

Price movements that happened before have a high chance of repeating themselves in the future. It is connected to the market psychology as the movements are the result of universal emotions like fear or excitement. TA uses this rule to predict possible outcomes based on how they played out in the past (this is where we include patterns and fractals, which we will cover shortly).

TA, in other words, is the analysis of the price movement. To do that, you can use various indicators, but the truth is that the simpler it is, the better. The more you are going to study, the more comfortable you will feel even without using all the available tools. Trading simple support and resistance zones can be as effective as using more advanced indicators, such as Ichimoku Cloud or Bollinger Bands.

During your analysis, you will have to spot both bullish and bearish signals and decide which side will prevail. Along with reading this chapter, we would highly recommend trying to play with the indicators as well (with one of the charting tools like TradingView or Coinigy. If you have never used them, we encourage watching few tutorials on YouTube before continuing). You will not be able to learn how to do it unless you try and fail several times first. Charting is a skill like any other, and therefore, if you do not practice, you will not be able to take real advantage of it.

There are few other concepts that we should cover here before we go into the analysis of the price action.

Trend

A trend is fundamental to anything related to TA. Every tool that we will be covering in this chapter will be used to study the trend and its strength further. Probably the number one rule in TA says, "Trend is your friend" which means you should not fight with it but trade with it. Let us give a small explanation of what it is exactly.

A trend is a direction in which the market is currently moving. It is a mixture of highs and lows that the price is making towards a particular direction. It is never a flat line but more like a series of waves that depending on where they find support and resistance, decide on the direction of the market. The interpretation of these price levels looks like this:

- Higher lows + higher highs – clear uptrend
- Lower lows + lower highs - clear downtrend

And

- Higher lows + lower highs – decreased volatility, preparing for a move
- Lower lows + higher highs – increased volatility, sideways

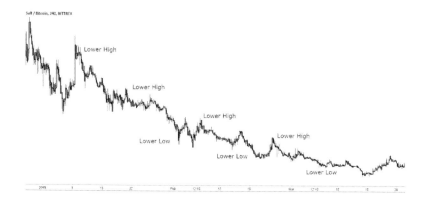

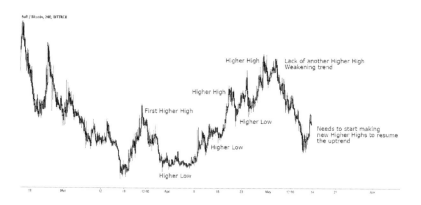

Therefore, as we can see, there are three types of a trend – uptrend, downtrend and horizontal trend (no clear direction). While the first two are obvious, the horizontal trend usually appears when the price is stabilising and preparing for the next move. There are not always enough signals out there that could predict whether the consolidation is going to break up or down, that is why sometimes the best trading decision is not to trade at all.

Very volatile price action with numerous spikes and dumps

(Trading Bitcoin in March 2018 was incredibly frustrating for many traders as there were no real indicators that could recommend taking either long or short position. We would usually call this a "no trade zone", and we would take the position only after the trend would be confirmed.)

A long-term trend is always more important than anything that is happening short-term. A multiyear uptrend stays bullish even if along the way several smaller downtrends serve the role of a correction. Playing on the market is nothing else but trying to catch that uptrend and sell before the downtrend starts. To do that, traders use various indicators that help them detect first signals of the trend reversal. In the following pages of this chapter, we will go through all the tools that in our opinion are the most effective in doing that.

Trading pairs

Each coin has its trading pair, sometimes few of them. Most currencies on the market are trading with BTC pairs – to buy them you first need to own part of Bitcoin. That makes them strictly correlated with Bitcoin so even if their price does not move, they can still gain or lose in USD value.

(Let's say we have a coin Tron that is worth 1000 satoshis. With BTC at 10k, it would translate to 0,01$ per coin (as 1000 satoshis equal 0.000001 BTC). Tron can gain or lose value in 2 ways – when it changes its BTC value and when Bitcoin changes its price. Let us present it by showing examples.

- *Tron stays at 1000 sat, but Bitcoin gained 2k, so it is now worth 12k. Tron despite staying on the same level is now worth 0,012$.*

- *Tron gained 50% with Bitcoin still at 10k. Tron is now worth 1500 sats, which translates into 0,015$ per coin.*

- *Tron gained 50%, but Bitcoin's value decreased by 50%. Tron is now worth 1500 sats and Bitcoin is worth 5k. This, despite the significant growth from the Tron, puts the coin at 0,0075$ price.)*

More and more currencies are currently being given few different pairs as well (ETH pairs, USDT (Tether) pairs etc.) but still a clear majority is highly correlated with Bitcoin. Until exchanges provide more USD pairs for the coins, all investors should always be aware of the BTC movements while trading their altcoins, as that affects them as well. When Bitcoin is very volatile, usually the whole market experiences significant drawbacks. Keep that in mind while trading and always look at Bitcoin chart in addition to the coin of your interest.

The general rule to picking a correct pair to chart would be to always go by the one with the biggest volume. Charts, in general, are more reliable when there is more liquidity in the market; therefore, you should be charting the most reliable pairing. This, however, does not mean that you should entirely dismiss the other pairs. Every chart shows a new perspective that should be taken into consideration.

(Even if a coin does not have an official USD/USDT pair, it is still worth charting the generated one (TradingView enables that option). As the chart is the reflection of the emotions and a lot of people trade based on USD value, this

serves as the additional perspective. Indecisiveness on the BTC chart might be explained easier with a breakout incoming on the USD chart. In the case when a coin has BTC and USD pairs in high volume, look at both of them but trade the one that interests you more (accumulating more BTC or USD).)

Log vs Linear

Type of scale that is being used during charting is also a topic of debate for many traders. It is hard to say that one is better than the other unequivocally, so we will try to explain in what situations we prefer to use either of them. Before that, however, we need a brief explanation of the scales themselves:

Linear – the distances between the prices are equal, no matter where they appear. A 10$ candle looks precisely the same at 20-30 range as it does at 410-420 range. The price is assessed purely by value (the gains equal 10$).

Logarithmic – the distances between the prices depend on the level they appear on. The same 10$ will look differently at 20-30 and 410-420 ranges as log charts measure the movement by their percentages (the gains equal 50% and 2,43% respectively).

350$ candle

In theory, log charts are more useful because they reflect the traders' emotions better, as the excitement is built on the percentage gain from the overall capital. It also allows the trader to analyse more volatile moves better as they are more proportional, instead of being almost vertical as it would be shown on linear charts.

In practice, however, we find success by using both, depending on the time frame. It is a very similar case to trading pairs – knowing both gives you more data to work with. For long-term setups, we prefer using logarithmic as it is more objective since it is not affected by the rapidness of the moves. Linear charts, however, tend to work better for us in the short-term setups as the breakouts are more evident and it is easier to evaluate the strength of the movement (potential blow-off tops or capitulation).

(An excellent example of both log and linear being in use could have been seen during recent (March 2018) breakout from the BTC diagonal downtrend. The first excitement came in when the price went past the resistance on the linear chart. Log-chart enthusiasts said this was a non-event as the resistance according to their setups was still far away. They turned out to be right as from the top of that breakout the price took another 45% dive before it decided to break through the log-trend on a much higher volume. The linear trendline was not respected at all during the downfall although it helped a great deal during assessing if 20k was the top for Bitcoin a few months earlier.)

However, this is still a matter of preference, and we encourage you to experiment with both types to see what brings better results for you.

Time frames

Picking a time frame depends on your approach to trading. If you are a day-trader, you will be looking at 1-hour or even 30-minute candles, while investors should usually be looking at higher time frames starting from daily (sometimes 4-hour candles). No matter what your choice is, you should realise that higher time frame always has the advantage over the lower one. If we receive mixed signals from 2 different time frames (let's say 1-hour and daily) the movement on the lower one is very short-term and serves as the correction to the more significant trend. When you are investing, you should always first zoom out to understand the overall trend direction and then start zooming in to find a potential entry as close to the support as possible.

While trading on lower time frames, you should not only remember that higher ones are more powerful, but you should also mark them in your setup. As we will shortly explain resistance and support zones, you will see how critical certain levels on the charts are for the price. Trading on daily candles alone can have good results, but for the full picture, you should also include important levels from both higher and lower time frames.

TA tools

Candles

The absolute basics of price action, candles, can be a much bigger help tool than most new traders realise. Only from them, it should be possible to analyse any chart along with projections on the future movements based on the shape of the candles alone. There are many different alternatives to candles (bars, lines, Heikin Ashi) but because of the basic character of this chapter, we will be covering the most popular one. This is how a candle is built:

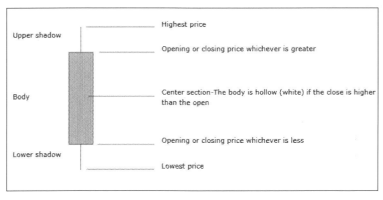

(The picture was taken from: http://www.wallstwise.com/Charting.htm)

The central part of the candle – the body – represents the opening and closure of the candle. The shadow (or wick) above and below it, shows how the price reached other levels before the candle's closure. A candle is the representation of the time frame – on a 1-hour time frame, a candle will represent 1 hour, on a 1-day time frame, a candle will represent one day and so on. If the price closes higher than it opens the candle is green (on our charts, white) and if the opposite happens, it turns red (on our charts, black).

The structure of the candle can tell a lot about the current trend. A long body with dominance over wicks is an indicator of strength, while long shadows and short body suggest trend weakness or potential reversal. The candles with long shadows are called dojis.

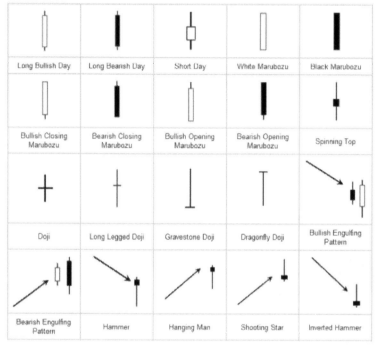

(The picture was taken from:
http://www.technicaltradingindicators.com/tradestation-indicators/83-candlestick-patterns/)

Depending on the time frame, a candle like Hammer or Shooting Star can be a clear reversal signal as it shows enormous buying/selling pressure on the coin. It does not require trendlines or other indicators to be able to project future moves, especially if the candle was formed on a daily time frame or higher.

Another very important single candle you will need is the one that appears during a blow-off top or capitulation. Those two are the reversal points in a trend, where the price makes an explosive move which then very quickly retraces. It is an indicator of a buying/selling climax that is followed by other people leaving or entering the market in an accelerated movement. A candle like this usually is massive and has a long wick which is later followed by another few candles that represent this accelerated buying/selling.

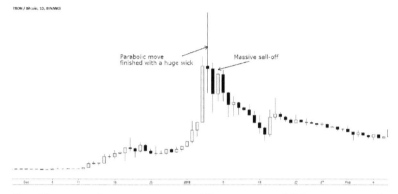

Candles can also create a specific pattern within a group of 2 or more, that also works as a great reversal or continuation signal. From the most popular ones, we would distinguish tweezer top/bottom and either Evening Doji Star or Morningstar. Those are reversal patterns that we personally often use to confirm our entries or exits.

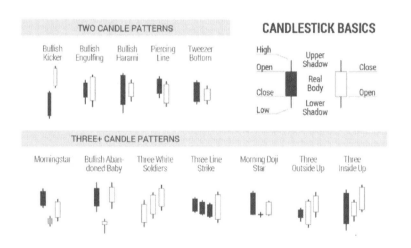

(The picture was taken from:
https://www.infographicsarchive.com/economics/candlesticks-cheat-sheet/)

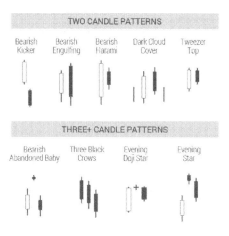

(The picture was taken from:
https://www.infographicsarchive.com/economics/candlesticks-cheat-sheet/*)*

Since we are trying to explain only the fundamental concept of candles, we will not go through every single pattern, as that misses the point of this chapter. At the end of this book, we provide resources to learn, so we encourage diving deep into them, once you are done with the book. Remember that candles are only one of the tools that can be used to predict the next moves, but it is essential to understand them as you will not always have access to more fancy indicators.

Resistance and support

When we were talking about trends, we mentioned that the price makes highs and lows that determine which way the market is going. Those levels are called resistance and support, and besides candles, they are the most important tool you will be using during your TA.

Support is the point where the prices bounce before going for a new high in an uptrend or another low in a downtrend. Broken support can indicate either a trend reversal (especially if it happens on a higher time frame) or a trend weakening but still with a chance of recovering on the next support. Resistance is the opposite of the support, as it represents a zone where selling pressure is higher than the buying one, forcing the price to retrace. A broken resistance is not instantly a signal for a new uptrend, but usually indicates at least the end of the downtrend (either uptrend continuation or starting a horizontal trend).

Fundamental rule to remember is that whenever support or resistance is breached, they change roles (broken support becomes resistance, and broken resistance becomes the support). It is essential not only in the later evaluation of how strong current level is but because very often that level is shortly tested. This usually serves a great spot to either buy or sell your position if you believe the trend is about to reverse.

The support and resistance can be drawn in 2 ways – either with horizontal levels or by trendlines. We will go through both as, once again, it is a matter of preference which one you will find more reliable. We know many traders who use only horizontals or only tradelines, and they are all experiencing massive success in the Cryptoworld. We prefer to mix both, as that gives us more tools to analyse charts with.

Horizontal

The first thing to understand about horizontals - or any support but with horizontals especially - is that these are not exact points. These are usually zones that range within certain amounts, and a short-term breach above or under can still be acknowledged as acting on that level if the price closes correctly.

A good horizontal level can be measured by:

- The number of touches - The more a particular zone was tested, the stronger it is.

- Reaction to the level - The more volatile the response is, the more strength it shows. If the bounce or rejection is significant, it should boost further confidence in that level.

- The number of flips - The more times this level acted as both resistance and support, the more significance it has (for both buyers and sellers).

- Time frame - If the zone was significant for more extended periods of time, it gains more importance.

- Recentness - The area should be tested from time to time to prove that it is still relevant.

As we mentioned earlier, it is good to mark those levels from the higher time frames down to the one you want to be trading on. If you're going to trade on 4H candles, you should mark Weekly and Daily levels as well. Let us show you how these levels would look like:

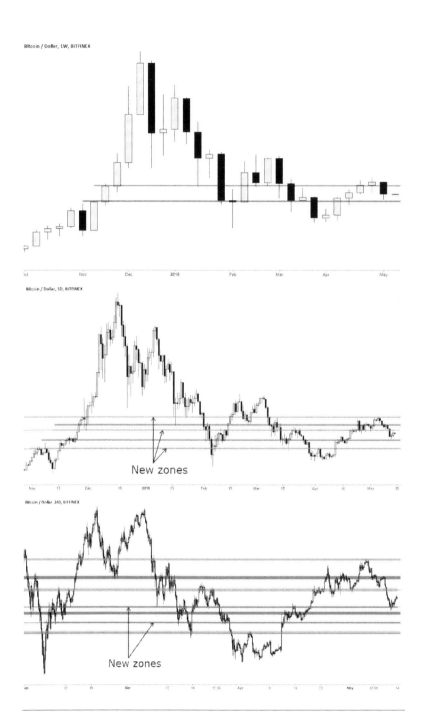

Bitcoin / Dollar, 1W, BITFINEX

Bitcoin / Dollar, 1D, BITFINEX

New zones

Bitcoin / Dollar, 240, BITFINEX

New zones

137

As you might have already noticed, many of these levels disregard the wicks of the candles. The reason for that is because the body is a much stronger indicator, especially if the wick is neither a top or a bottom of the price range. The wicks are often the result of stop hunts (market makers moving the price to trigger stop-losses) or low liquidity pumps. For that reason, they should be valued but not above the bodies of the candles.

Most of those levels were also simple lines and not zones, as mentioned earlier. That is because the zones should be created in the areas where those lines are really close to each other. Precision is critical in TA when you want to get the best entries and exits possible; therefore, you should try avoiding drawing zones too broad, as they will have less value.

When it comes to trading these levels, it is very simple. The price movements are ranges between support and resistance. Your job as a trader is to buy at support and sell at resistance, depending on how strong it is. When trading daily candles, you can ignore resistance from 4H time frame as it would limit your profits. You should not, however, ignore the higher time frame levels as they do not lose their value.

Using only horizontal levels can lead to very successful setups, especially if you connect them with candle patterns and other indicators. Let's look at how we could use the alternative version of support and resistance in trendlines.

Trendlines

The same as with horizontals, we will start with the measures of a good trendline:

-   The number of touches - A good trendline has at least three touches, but you can draw a more speculative one with two as well. It will not be a mistake; it is just the importance that is a bit lower than in the case of lines with more touching points.

- Spread - The touch points should be spread out across the trendline and not focused on one area. If that happens, there is a high chance that it will not be valid if further extended.

- Length - The longer the trendline is with frequent touches, the more significant it is to the trend.

- Time frame - Higher time frame always produces more important trendlines than the lower ones.

Drawing trendlines should be done by connecting high or low points of the movement, depending on whether you are trying to show support or resistance. It is essential that neither of those lines is breached by the price because otherwise, the trendline is in most cases invalid (some trendlines do work inside of the chart, but they require a significant amount of touches). Drawing usually should focus on the wicks, but you should not be afraid to cut through some of them if the trendline appears legitimate anyway.

You can, of course, draw the same lines focusing mostly on the bodies of the candles; there is no hard rule to this. The main point is that the trendline should meet all the criteria listed earlier. Same as with horizontals, trendlines can be breached and turned into the opposite (support to resistance and vice versa); therefore, we would suggest not to delete them even if they broke up or down.

The same as with horizontals, the break of one support should lead the price to the next one. In regular TA, you could be using horizontal level here to show the next support, but let's say we want to use only trendlines. During more rapid movements, it is recommended to adjust your current setup to the chart. This means that if the price is increasing faster than the line suggests, you should create a new one that would fit with the dynamic of the movement. A break of such trendline would put the next bounce target at the previous line.

0x / Bitcoin, 240, BINANCE

Trading these levels gives a couple of possibilities. Trendlines are commonly used in popular patterns, that we will be covering shortly, but they can also be used solely as the resistance and support in the channels.

IOSToken / Bitcoin, 240, BINANCE

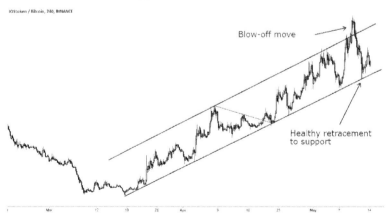

Trendlines are also helpful in discovering divergences which we will discuss in the Oscillators segment. It is essential always to try to confirm one tool with another. A perfect way of doing that can be seen in patterns and volume that is accompanying them.

Patterns

We have mentioned before that one of the primary rules of TA is that the history tends to repeat itself. Patterns are proof of that assumption, as they tend to happen frequently presenting very similar results each time. Each pattern has its own structure and a measured outcome although by no means they should be taken for granted. Each pattern, even if very clear, needs to be first confirmed and often matched with a fitting volume profile (more on volume in the next segment). If it is not paired with a suiting volume, it still might be valid, but the probability of it playing out is much smaller.

Patterns can take a lot of different shapes such as triangles, rectangles, wedges and couple of others. They can be divided into three main categories – continuation, bilateral and reversal patterns. Let us focus on the last one first.

Reversal patterns indicate the change of a trend, depending on the time frame. A pattern that appears on 1H candles does not mean the reversal for the long-term trend, but simply points at the start of the correction. As with any other indicator, the higher the time frame, the more significant a particular pattern is. The two most popular reversal patterns out there are double top and Head and Shoulders. This works for both the top and the bottom as those can be inverted as well (like a mirror image).

The fundamental rule here is that the pattern is invalid until it is confirmed (in case of H&S its neckline must be crossed). Trading it before the confirmation is risky and therefore should be backed by other indicators as well. Otherwise, there is a high possibility of a bounce, which was often seen during recent (April 2018) BTC movements.

As we mentioned, each pattern has a measured outcome once it is confirmed. Very often it is the distance from the base support to the highest point of the pattern, but that varies depending on the type. This outcome should not be taken for granted as the target often gets halted by a strong support/resistance on the way to it; therefore, it should be traded accordingly to the other zones mapped on the chart.

Here is a small cheat sheet of available reversal patterns (there are a lot more, but these are most common. We encourage to learn in more details about any of them from the materials we are providing at the end of this book):

Reversal Patterns

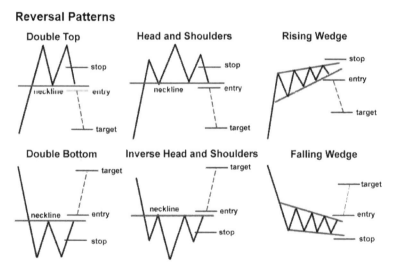

(The picture was taken from: https://www.forexboat.com/3-best-chart-patterns-for-intraday-trading-in-forex/reversal-forex-chart-patterns-cheat-sheet/)

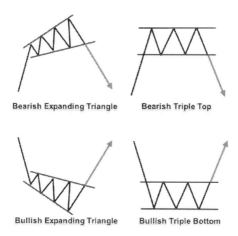

Bearish Expanding Triangle	Bearish Triple Top

Bullish Expanding Triangle	Bullish Triple Bottom

(The picture was taken from: https://www.forexboat.com/3-best-chart-patterns-for-intraday-trading-in-forex/reversal-forex-chart-patterns-cheat-sheet/)

Head and Shoulders

Formed by two peaks and a higher one in between, with a neckline connecting two low points from the "shoulders". This line is often a slope and usually is more reliable if it is pointing down. This pattern is valid after the neckline is breached and the target is measured by taking the distance from the neckline to the top of the head.

Double Top/Bottom

Similar to Head and Shoulder but with only two peaks that get rejected at the same resistance level. It is also valid only if the neckline is breached and the target is measured from the base to the top of the movement. The pattern has other variations in the shape of triple bottom/top, but they are less frequent.

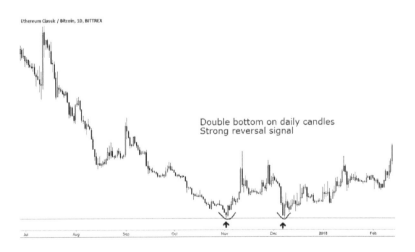

Wedges

Wedges can act as both reversal and continuation patterns, depending on their previous trend (uptrend with a rising wedge – reversal. Downtrend with a rising wedge – continuation). It is a consolidation period where both slopes are pointing in the same direction. The target is measured by the height of the movement from the breakout point.

Rising wedge – higher highs with even higher lows. It is a bearish pattern, but sometimes during a strong uptrend, it tends to break upwards as well.

Falling wedge – lower highs with even lower lows. A bullish pattern, also very common as a continuation signal.

Bilateral patterns

Bilateral patterns are a little bit trickier because they do not point in a definite direction. In this category, we list the triangles that have a similar chance of breaking out in both ways. In deciding which course is more possible, we should be considering current trend and strength of the other indicators that could point us to the more probable outcome.

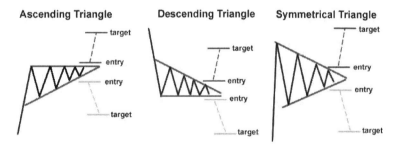

(The picture was taken from: https://tresorfx.com/breakout-technical-analysis/)

Triangles

We can distinguish three types of triangles. They are measured from the bottom of the structure to the top of it. The outcome is that exact measurement counted from the breakout point. Keep in mind that each one of them can go either direction even if the structure points to being more bullish/bearish:

Ascending Triangle – making higher lows with a flat resistance top. This is the most bullish structure as it signals increasing buying pressure.

Descending Triangle – making lower lows with flat support. The opposite of ascending triangle, this is a bearish setup that shows buyers weakness to defend their support.

Symmetrical Triangle – making higher lows and lower highs. This setup is the most neutral of all triangles, and its outcome should be suggested by the trend it appears in.

Continuation patterns

Before we get to the regular continuation patterns, we should mention that there are cases where reversal patterns can act as such as well. It is not very common but if the volume profile fits they should not be disregarded and can be traded accordingly to the direction they point at.

Continuation patterns serve the role of a small consolidation period in a clear trend that is likely to continue going the same direction. Just like reversal patterns those as well need to be first formed and confirmed by a breakout to be considered valid. We can divide this category into pennants, rectangles and wedges (which work here the same way as we mentioned them previously, that is why we will only show the example).

Continuation Patterns

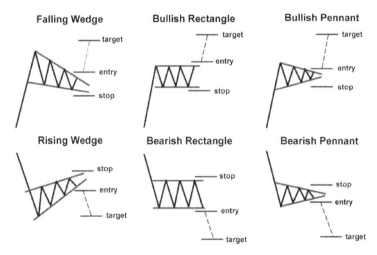

(The picture was taken from: https://www.forexboat.com/3-best-chart-patterns-for-intraday-trading-in-forex/continuation-forex-chart-patterns-cheat-sheet/)

Pennants

Pennants are very similar to triangles but are shorter in duration and appear after a very rapid move. The outcome should be measured from the pole they created to the top of the formation. They should be traded with caution as they appear mostly during massive pumps or dumps.

Pennants can also take the shape of an angled rectangle, which then we would call a flag. The measurement is done the same way, but the consolidation is within two parallel lines and not a triangle.

Rectangles

Rectangles are consolidation zones where the price is trapped between two parallel lines in a clear trend. The price tends to test both support and resistance few times before continuing. The breakout direction usually follows the previous move, and the target is measured by the height of the box from the breakout point.

Litecoin / Bitcoin, 15, BINANCE

Volume

Volume is one of the best strength indicators out there. It is a measurement of how much a given coin was traded during a specific period. The more volume there is in a particular market, the bigger liquidity is, therefore it is easier to enter/exit or day-trade. It is mostly used to evaluate if the current price action is valid and helps in confirming reversals and breakouts.

Volume profiles look differently in an uptrend and downtrend. They present as follows:

Uptrend – volume increasing along with the price, declining when the price dips

Downtrend – volume increasing when the price falls, and decreasing when it raises

Volume increasing with price

Low volume on retracement

Volume spike on uptrend continuation

Increasing volume on bigger moves, decreasing on bounces

When the price is making new highs with the volume being lower than on the previous spikes, it is an indicator of decreasing buying pressure and possible retracement. This should be traded carefully and possibly confirmed with other tools if the trend really is weakening.

DigiByte / Bitcoin, 240, POLONIEX
Vol

Decreasing buying volume on each spike

This confirms one of the primary rules of volume – volume proceeds the price. Whether it is decreasing buying pressure on a new high, or increasing one while the price is still stable, the volume gives signals about upcoming price action. It should be watched closely during consolidation period for some accumulation signals as they can be very visible on low liquidity markets (some coins manage to do 3/4/5x while still being only on few BTC value volume).

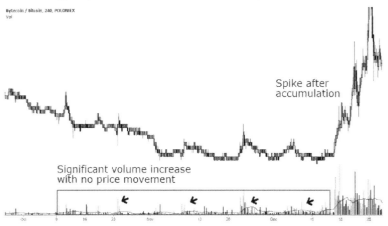

Bytecoin / Bitcoin, 240, POLONIEX
Vol

Spike after accumulation

Significant volume increase with no price movement

Volume also works as a pattern confirmation as we mentioned in the earlier segment. Every pattern has the volume profile that makes it more probable. On bullish pennant, this means decreasing volume during the consolidation, while on Head and Shoulders the buying volume is diminishing with each peak and increasing on the neckline breach.

Volume also decides if the breakout from the pattern is not a possible fake-out. What it means is that often the price tends to convincingly escape the pattern just to reverse and go the opposite direction quickly. It is a way of trapping traders that can be easily avoided by watching volume during the breakout. If it is low, there is a very high chance that you are dealing with a fake-out, which will see an increased volume spike shortly while going the opposite way. If it is high during the breakout, the pattern usually is valid and will continue its movement direction.

Fake-out is a term that applies not only to patterns, but any price movement that goes the opposite direction as the setup would suggest. Depending on which way the price decides to go this move is also called either a bull trap (upwards move followed by a dump) or a bear trap (downwards move followed by a pump).

An alternative to the regular volume is the On-Balanced Volume (OBV) tool that measures total buying and selling pressure on the market. It works accordingly to all the rules that we listed in this segment, i.e. volume rising along with the price, volume proceeding the price etc.

OBV can be analysed with support/resistance zones like any other chart. If the OBV is in uptrend along with the price, the breakdown of the trend suggests a drop in price as well. As the volume proceeds the price, the divergences occurring on the OBV also often point at the potential upcoming reversal.

Divergence – a situation where the price and indicator are moving in different directions. It can be either positive or negative depending on the direction of the movements. It shows either a trend weakening or gaining more momentum.

Bullish divergence – lower lows in price, higher lows on the indicator. Bearish trend is weakening.

Hidden Bullish divergence – higher lows in price, lower lows on the indicator. The bullish trend is getting stronger.

Bearish divergence – higher highs in price, lower highs on the indicator. The bullish trend is weakening.

Hidden bearish divergence – lower highs in price, higher highs on the indicator. Bearish trend is getting stronger.

Divergence Cheat Sheet

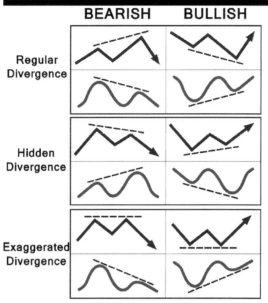

(The picture was taken from https://www.forexfactory.com/showthread.php?t=557434)

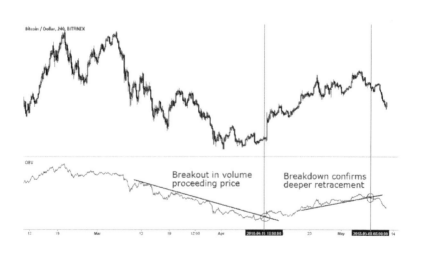

It is a very simple tool that often shows signals, which would be hard to spot on a regular volume. As always, we suggest using it with other indicators for more confirmation, but it is a valuable tool to any trader's arsenal.

Fractals

Another example of how history tends to repeat itself is a frequent appearance of fractals. Fractals are nothing else but patterns that already happened before, therefore making them more probable to appear again in the future. An excellent example of those are all the patterns that we listed in the previous segments (triangles etc.) or overall market cycles that we will explain in the next chapter. The fractals are in no way a standalone system and they should be used with other tools. Just because a particular pattern happened before, does not mean it is primed to repeat. The market fundamentals are often very different in both situations that is why fractals should be only used as the ideas that are worth exploring further.

The use of fractals is pretty loose and depends highly on a trader. The more indicators are matching in both scenarios, the higher the chance is of the fractal repeating. There is no real limit on what tools could be used here – resistance/support, fibs, EMAs – everything that we will cover in this chapter could serve as a fractal confirmation. As they can apply to both smaller and bigger scales, do not be afraid to compare stock to Cryptocurrencies as well.

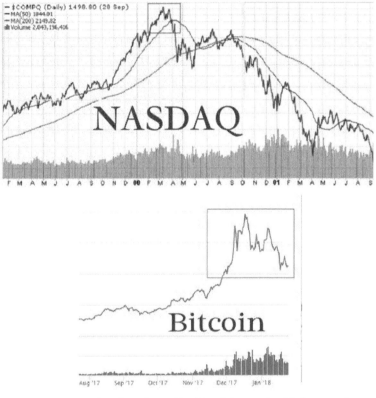

(The picture was taken from https://seekingalpha.com/article/4140126-bitcoin-will-fall-1000)

Fibs

We will not be getting into the origins of Fibonacci ratios as we only want to focus on how traders can benefit from them. Your charting software is going to calculate them for you anyway. Fibs (we will be using this shortcut) are one of the primary tools in every trader's arsenal as they are used to point out entry and exit areas. Before we explain how to use Fibonacci ratios we need to present the definitions of swing low and swing high.

Swing high – a candlestick with two lower highs on the side

Swing low – a candlestick with the higher lows on the side

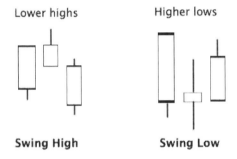

(The picture was taken from:
https://www.forexfactory.com/showthread.php?t=411874)

Using Fibs relies on finding those two candlesticks that would indicate the start and the end of the trend we would like to measure. If it is an upwards move we will start measuring from the swing low and end on the swing high. If it is a downwards move we measure it from the swing high to the swing low. It is usually recommended to use the wicks of the candle, but if it is overextended (by maybe a pump and dump group), you can also start from the nearest body close. There are no strict rules on which swings you should be picking – this is what makes Fibs very individual for every trader. The only thing we would recommend is that the measurement should be obvious, as it should start from the clear bottom and end on a clear top for that specific rally.

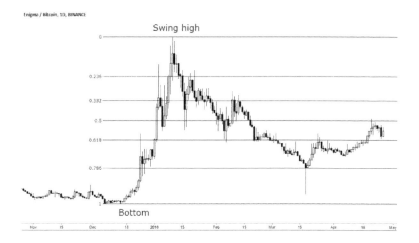

If we would like to find a support/resistance, we would be using Fibonacci retracement levels, while looking at potential profit taking zones would require using Fibonacci extensions. Let's go through both cases.

Finding support

Finding support and resistance looks basically the same, with a difference of starting the fibs either from the swing low or swing high. The discover the support zones, we should be drawing them from the swing low and finishing at the swing high which would give us few potential bounce zones.

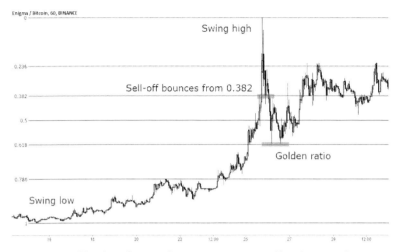

However, fibs by themselves are not as effective as they are with the addition of other supports in the same area. You should not bet on a price bouncing from a spot only because there is an important fib level there – you should connect those areas to horizontal or diagonal supports so that they are more significant for the price.

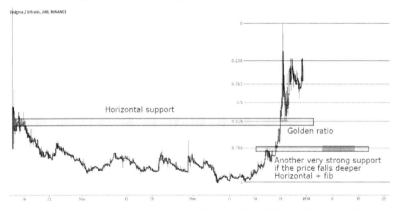

In theory, the most important level should be the 0.618 as it is a "golden ratio" of the Fibonacci theory. Especially after a more significant move, the retracements tend to be deeper, therefore look at this spot to have a bigger effect on the price.

Finding resistance

All the rules that we just mentioned apply to resistances as well. With a difference of drawing from the top to the bottom, fibs can also be used to find potential resistance zones.

Those levels do not always react with the price as well; therefore, it is recommended to look at those overlapping with other resistances.

Finding profit taking zones

In case of many coins that do not have a rich price history or because they are approaching ATH it is hard for traders to determine what should be their next target. That is where we suggest using Fibonacci extensions which show potential profit taking zones when there are no more resistances in sight.

We draw Fibonacci extensions the same way as we would measure it while looking for resistance zones. We do it from swing high to swing low and this way additional zones will appear above the 1 level of the swing high's wick. Same as with 0.618 fib for retracements, the 1.618 level for extensions also serves as the strongest area of importance.

A small note before we proceed to the Ichimoku Cloud – fibs can and should be used on different time frames just like we did it with horizontals. What we mean is that when you are charting 4-hour candles, try first drawing the fibs on a daily time frame as that gives you additional zones to look at. Higher time frames are always more significant; therefore, it will make your current setup more complete.

Ichimoku Cloud

Ichimoku Cloud is an incredibly complex topic that would not match with a beginner's knowledge explained in this chapter; therefore, we will only cover the basics. Before we begin, you need to know that Ichimoku has different settings in Cryptocurrencies, as the market works 24/7. For that reason, instead of regular settings, we are using 20/60/120/30. If you are charting alongside this chapter, make sure you adjust your cloud to those. It is also worth noting that Ichimoku works best on the coins with previous price history. Therefore, if the data is not sufficient, you can use the 10/30/60/30 settings that improve the effectiveness.

The Cloud should be used when the trend is visible to help determine entry and exit targets. It does not work during the horizontal trend and consolidation as the indicators often give false signals. There are a few things that Ichimoku includes:

We are mostly going to focus on Kijun and Kumo for determining good entry and exit spots, but keep in mind that there are a lot more use cases to the Ichimoku apart from what we are going to present. Our list of the most important indicators is the following:

TK Cross

TK Cross occurs when Tenkan crosses either below (bearish) or above Kijun (bullish). Depending on the position of the cross in relation to the Kumo, this gives different signals for a trader. If we were considering taking either a long or short position on Bitcoin, we would interpret them this way:

- A bullish cross above the cloud – powerful buying signal, open a long position.

- A bearish cross above the cloud – a sign of a weakening trend. Not a short signal yet, but probably a good place to close the long.

- A bullish cross below the cloud – similarly, not a long signal yet, but closing a short should be considered here. The trend is showing weakness.

- A bearish cross below the cloud – very bearish signal, the trend is getting stronger. Open a short position.

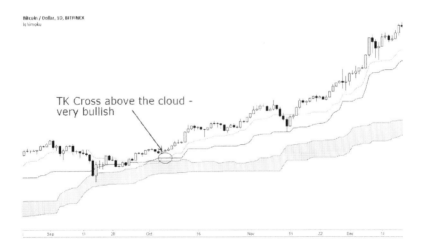

Kumo&Kijun support and resistance

Both Kijun and Kumo cloud can be used as the support and resistance zones. For Kumo, those zones are on both edges, not only on the closer one to the price. If the price manages to break up through the cloud, it is a bullish signal, the same way it is bearish if the Kumo does not manage to hold the price as support.

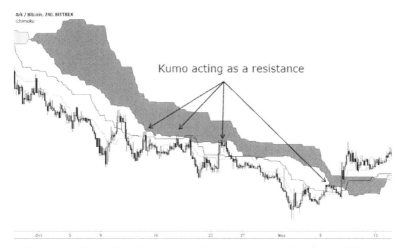

Kijun, on the other hand, can be viewed as the overall trend support/resistance. In a strong uptrend buying on Kijun is the equivalent of buying horizontal or diagonal support. As the trend often accelerates, Kijun tends to drift away from the price, which is a signal of a possible pullback incoming (Ichimoku likes to have everything in equilibrium).

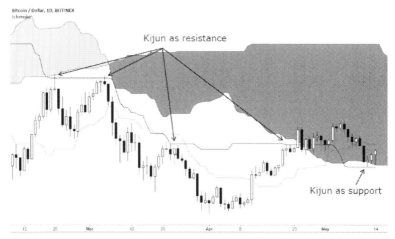

As Kijun serves the role of the trend's main line, a price cross below or above should serve as a strong signal as well. As with almost any other indicator, the higher the time frame, the more significant that cross is.

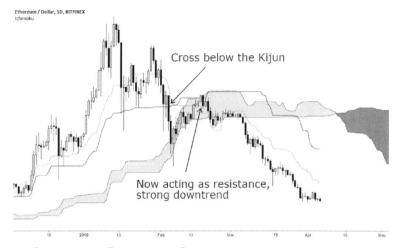

Ethereum / Dollar, 1D, BITFINEX
Ichimoku

Cross below the Kijun

Now acting as resistance, strong downtrend

Edge to Edge Trades

When the price enters a Kumo cloud and manages to close a candle inside, very often, it tends to test the opposite edge. The buying signal would be at the close of the candle at the beginning of the cloud, and the bigger the cloud it, the higher reward potentially awaits. Not always the price goes straight through the middle of Kumo to reach the opposite edge, as that often takes some movement inside of it as well. That, however, does not change the target, so if you can find other indicators confirming the strength of the trend, those trades tend to have a good risk/reward ratio.

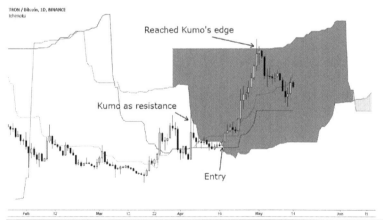

TRON / Bitcoin, 1D, BINANCE
Ichimoku

Reached Kumo's edge

Kumo as resistance

Entry

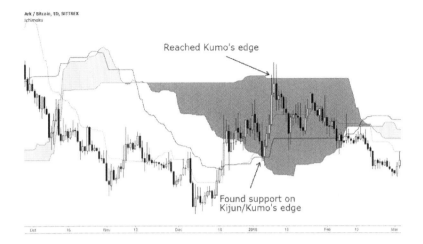

Ark / Bitcoin, 1D, BITTREX

Reached Kumo's edge

Found support on
Kijun/Kumo's edge

Kumo Twist

Senkou Spans (Kumo edges in other words) can give a lot of
signals to a trader when they twist. The simplest one that we
like to take into the consideration is the colour of the cloud
that we look at before taking a position. The twist can either
support or reject the idea of buying a coin at the current spot
– if it turns red, it points at the trend weakening giving more
of a sell signal than anything else. The opposite holds true as
well if the twist occurs turning Kumo green. Keep in mind
that this should never be a deciding factor in you taking a
trade, but only a small addition to the other signals you are
receiving from the chart.

Ripple / Dollar, 1D, BITFINEX
Ichimoku

Opening long position now is not recommended

TK Cross

Kumo twist

Price below the cloud

TK Disequilibrium

Ichimoku Cloud can also be used as an oscillator thanks to the Tenkan and Kijun lines. As Ichimoku prefers everything in equilibrium, the spread between those two lines can be seen as an oversold or overbought signal. If the price tends to accelerate too much, the distance between these two increases, giving a signal to the trader that the correction might be incoming. This is also only one of many indicators that should never be traded alone, but keep it in mind if the significant disparity appears.

Bitcoin / Dollar, 1D, BITFINEX
Ichimoku

Gap getting bigger

Gap getting bigger

Correction

Moving Averages

Moving average is another tool that helps to indicate the current trend and confirm its reversal. While prices can often be very volatile, the moving average smooths out the noise and presents the trend in the form of a simple line. There are a lot of different MAs that we can use (SMA, WMA, EMA) and they can also be divided by how much data they cover (50-day, 100-day, 200-day moving averages). For shorter trades, we recommend EMAs as they respond to the price much quicker, while Simple Moving Averages are more reliable for long-term analysis. For shorter periods you can use 10 and 20-day averages as well.

With a single line, a price below the MA is considered to be in a downtrend and with a price above it – in an uptrend. It also acts as a support/resistance but be careful if you are planning your buys or sells based on them alone. Moving average is a lagging indicator, which means that it is based on past prices and is intended to confirm the trend, not predict it. To consider EMA is acting as a support in short-term it first needs to test it, same with being a resistance. Moving average can be used as a signal to buy/sell but is not always the most reliable indicator, especially on lower time frames.

On a long-term time frame, like any other indicator, moving averages are more significant, especially if you add crosses to it. When you have 2 MAs they often tend to cross each other just like Tenkan and Kijun lines did in Ichimoku Cloud. When a faster moving average crosses above the slower one, it is a bullish signal. If the opposite happens (a faster one crosses below slower one) it is a bearish signal. The leading two averages that confirm trend reversal are 50-day and 200-day MAs. When 50 breaks below 200 we have a so-called "Death Cross" which means the downtrend, and when breaks above 200 we have a "Golden Cross" which indicated the bullish trend.

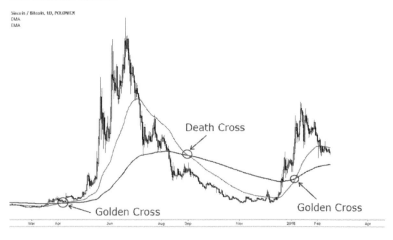

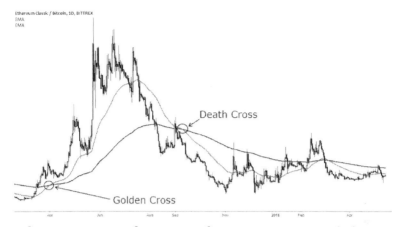

Whenever a cross happens, of any two averages, it is very often already too late to enter a position, since as we said it is a lagging indicator. To stay ahead of the cross, we suggest using other indicators that could point at the trend reversal as well, when the two averages are narrowing the gap between them. As with every other trade, never rush into it but wait for the best entry possible even if it means missing the potential profits.

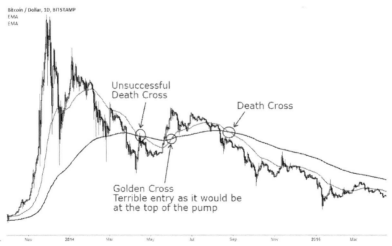

Oscillators

Oscillators are extremely helpful as they can be used to predict potential reversal and analyse current market condition. They are tools that are closed between two values which allow seeing whether the market is overbought or oversold.

Overbought – buyers are exhausted, the price has experienced a prolonged uptrend without a significant correction. RSI is above 70.

Oversold – sellers are exhausted, the price has sharply fallen, and the bounce is expected. RSI is below 30.

We are going to focus on three main oscillators – RSI, Stochastic RSI and MACD. All of them have a very similar function, but each one can be benefited from differently.

RSI

RSI – Relative Strength Index – is used to measure the speed and change of the price movements. The RSI has its overbought levels set at 70 and oversold at 30. It is recommended, that during the bear markets the lower level should be at 20, and during a bull market, the upper one should be at 80. This, however, is not necessary and using standard settings is appropriate as well. Knowing only this, the RSI can already give us few signals:

- Price crosses from below 30 upwards – possible buy signal and the start of a new uptrend. A good spot to close short positions.

- Price dips from above 70 downwards – possible sell signal and the beginning of the retracement. A good place to close long positions.

As always never make your decision based only on one indicator and try to confirm it with different tools as well.

RSI can also just like OBV be analysed with regular trendlines. The rules here are the same – whenever RSI breaks the trendline, we can expect a start of a different trend. In that case, the level that should be carefully watched is the middle line at 50. This one works either as resistance or support, depending from which side it is approached, and it often indicates how strong the current trend is (whether it is breached easily or if it manages to stop the line).

The most effective use of RSI in our opinion lies in previously mentioned divergences. They are used to discover hidden signals that the price itself is not showing and greatly help in finding possible reversal spots. Since we already explained what the types of divergences are, we will prove the effectiveness of this method by a couple of examples.

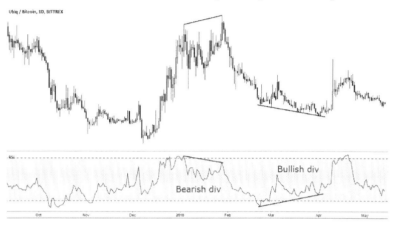

Stochastic RSI

StochRSI is a very simple indicator, that is mostly used to assess how close the current trend is to the reversal. The classic settings set the StochRSI between to values of 20 and 80, which are the overbought/oversold levels that should be watched. If the values reach above 80 or below 20, this should serve as a signal for an upcoming pullback or bounce, depending which value was crossed. In Cryptocurrencies, however, during extremely bullish/bearish conditions those levels can remain very irrational for more extended periods of time. That is why it is not suggested to use this indicator as a standalone system.

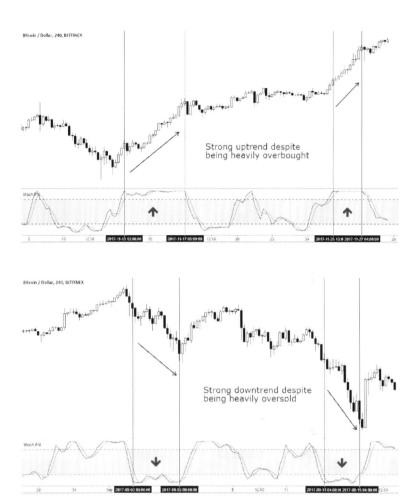

Divergences also occur on StochRSI, and they work the same way they do on the regular RSI. They are, however, less frequent as this indicator is more extreme, and it reaches its maximum or minimum values more often. On certain occasions, it can provide additional value to the analysis.

StochRSI should not be traded based on overbought/oversold levels alone. Use this indicator to confirm the weakness or strength of the trend by other tools, but taking actions based on overbought/oversold levels alone are not suggested due to irrationality of the market.

MACD

MACD consists of a histogram and two moving averages (here we have 12 and 26-day MAs). The signals from it can be read by either crossovers or divergences, and the results are like those at RSI. The cross of the two lines gives the buy/sell signals, just like it is happening with MAs (fast MA above slower one is bullish, slower MA above faster one is bearish). Analysing MACD by the overbought/oversold levels works identically to the StochRSI.

The interesting part with MACD starts with analysing divergences alongside the histogram. On the MAs they work the same way as they can be seen in OBV and RSI; therefore, we will not explain it once again.

The histogram, however, brings additional value as it can also show a trend weakening or getting stronger. This indicator made of vertical poles represents the disparity between the MAs. The histogram can dip below or rise above its 0 line that reflects how much is the disparity between the MAs increasing or decreasing. If it is below and comes closer to the middle line, it means that the trend is weakening (same happens the other way around). Crossing over this 0 line could be used as a buy/sell signal, but it is too unreliable to be used alone, therefore as always, we suggest matching it with other indicators.

Bollinger Bands

Bollinger Bands are one of our favourite tools to predict upcoming volatility in the coin. It consists of a moving average in the middle and two trading bands outside of it that expand and contract based on the previous price action. Bollinger Bands are not a standalone system, and they need to be traded with other indicators to be effective.

There are two ways to trade Bollinger bands – treat the bands as the local support/resistance or prepare for the upcoming strong move.

Majority of the price action that occurs takes place inside of the outer bands. The moving average in the middle often acts as local support and resistance, while the outer bands reflect overbought/oversold levels that could be a signal to buy or sell.

(If we are buying a lower band, the price target is first the MA in the middle, and once it crosses, the target becomes the upper band. Same goes the other way.)

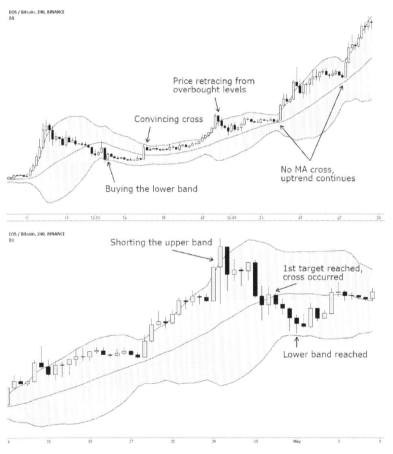

Every price breakout outside of the bands is considered a major move, which causes the bands to expand significantly. If the candles tend to close outside of those bands or even start opening there, it is a signal of a majorly extended price action that should see a retracement shortly.

Bollinger bands are not a standalone system, because even if the bands are tightening, there is still a need to asses in which way the price is more likely to go. A tightening of bands is an excellent indicator of an upcoming movement, but it needs to be confirmed with other tools such as divergences. Especially on higher time frames, an identified uptrend with a squeezed Bollinger Bands might serve as a great entry before a major breakout. This is often met at the bottom after an extended consolidation period when the coin is about to start a new long-term uptrend.

A small note before we proceed to the order book – the default settings for Bollinger Bands is 20, but with Cryptocurrencies being a 24/7 market, it might make sense to trade them on the 30. This way more data is captured and the tool is more precise, although we have found a lot of success by trading in the standard setting as well. Experiment with both and see which one serves you better.

Order book

The order book is a list of bids (buy orders) and asks (sell orders) on the market of a particular coin. It shows the buying and selling pressure on the market, which gives a clearer picture of what we could expect from the upcoming moves in the short-term.

There is a problem however with order books in Cryptocurrencies, because the market is heavily manipulated. We will explain it in the next chapter how whales can influence the order book to scare people, but even without them, the crypto markets are very prone to bot manipulation. That alone makes the order books not a real reflection of the current market state and basing your trades on that can have bad consequences. However, there is a way in which we utilise order books with success.

In a very short-term when we want to exit or enter our position, we tend to look at the order structure and the volume. Outside of the TA and potential support/resistance, we are looking where the biggest orders are set and how possible it is to fulfil them with the current volume (assuming it is not a fake wall set by a big player). If the order book is too thick to reach our preferable position, we tend to sometimes place our orders just outside of them. This way we might not get the perfect selling/buying point, but at least we have a higher chance of filling our position in a spot close enough anyway.

(If you have a coin with 20 BTC daily volume, it might be tough to get past through the asks worth even 4 or 5 BTC. If we would like to unload our position quickly we would set our sell order just next to the significant asks, which lowers profitability a bit but significantly increases the chances of our orders getting filled.)

TA Tips:

- Never sell or buy in a panic. Even if you did not manage to sell the top or buy the bottom, wait for the pullback to realise your position. Every rapid move will see a small bounce.

- Trade accordingly to what the chart is giving you, not what your bias suggests. It is extremely easy to get caught up in seeing bullish patterns if we like the project. Always try approaching the charts without any emotions, do not get attached to your coin.

- If you miss a good entry, do not FOMO into it. There are so many opportunities on the market you will find another one if the previous one did not work out.

- Try to learn from other traders but do not blindly follow them. It is good to search for inspiration, but nothing can beat a system that works for you.

- When starting, try trading on big time frames (from 1D to even 1W). They are more accurate and less risky for inexperienced traders.

- Use simple TA – the fewer indicators you will be using, the quicker you will learn to read any price action. In no situation, you should ever need a specific group of tools to be able to analyse the chart. They should act as a tool for help, but not as a necessity as simple candles are more than enough to explain previous movements and assess current trend strength.

- Do not get discouraged after few failures. Every trader has a losing streak where every single setup fails. It is important to be persistent and stick to your strategy (under the condition that it was successful before). If you do not believe in your own charts, you will find yourself going by somebody else's which will significantly limit you as a trader.

Finally, we would like to present a list of things-to-do, when approaching TA of a particular coin. You can treat this as a cheat sheet.

Choose the pair and time frame - Check the trading pair with the most volume and choose your time frame (we recommend looking at daily first even if you are in for a quick swing. This allows you to see the overall trend). Analyze the chart on the exchange with the most volume as well.

Draw support and resistance - Find the support and resistance zones. Check the point of the trend the price is currently in.

Analyze potential patterns and volume - Check if any popular patterns are forming that could predict the next move. Along with that, analyse the volume to confirm the legitimacy of the pattern/current movement.

Look for additional signals by using indicators - To confirm further your trade idea, use indicators that would support your claim. Look for divergences, squeeze on BBands or EMA crosses. Decide whether the existing signals are enough to take a trade.

Set your orders - Do not market buy but place your buy/sell orders on the resistance/support of your choice. Leave the orders to get filled. If that does not happen, look for another opportunity. If you set buy orders, do not forget to create stop-losses as well (we will cover them in the next chapter).

Up to this point, you should be able to evaluate projects on their short and long-term potential from both a fundamental and technical perspective. It is now time for us to show you how to apply the theory you learned in trading.

Investment strategies

What would your skills in FA and TA be worth if you did not know how to protect your capital or allocate your coins? Without a proper trading strategy, they would mean absolutely nothing. A good exit is not only a sell order at the nearest resistance – you need to know where to put those profits after the trade and how to protect yourself in case the next trade does not work out. In this chapter we will cover everything from understanding market cycles to timing entries at the bottom, taking profits at the top and sustaining the money made, using a well-balanced portfolio.

A small note before we begin – every trader has a different strategy that suits their needs and risk tolerance. In this chapter, we gathered the methods that work for us and our fellow traders, that allowed us to stay profitable in this market through all the volatility it experiences. You will not, however, find a definite answer on what is the best way to trade, since that is something each person must discover individually. First, understand what it means to have proper risk management and build your portfolio correctly from the start, but be prepared that only real experience can show you what suits you best in trading.

(We can surely say that we do not know one single trader that did not fail before finding success in trading. You can be profitable at the beginning but fail at preserving the capital which would lead you to point zero anyway because you lacked the experience to resist the greed. We are not indicating that you are destined to lose money before you can get successful – we mean that no long-term profitability is possible before you experience every part of investing including suffering loss, which is an integral part of trading.)

General knowledge

Market cycles

There are two things certain in the Cryptocurrency market – volatility and the fact that you will see this chart at least three times a day if you are on Twitter:

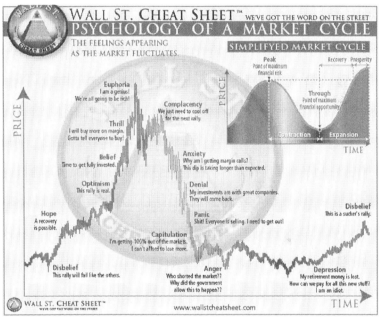

The picture was taken from: http://kazonomics.com/the-truth-of-btc-episode-3-the-invisible-hand-of-belarus/)

This image shows the classical visualisation of a market cycle. It is a representation of the coin's lifecycle and emotions that are met during certain stages of it. The reason why it is so popular is that it perfectly applies to the crypto market as the volatility significantly speeds up price action.

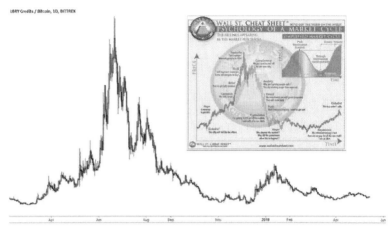

If you would go through most of the top 100 coins with price history going further than 2017, you would probably see at least 2 or 3 of those. Some smaller, some with more extended accumulation periods but still sharing a very similar pattern: a strong run finished by a blow-off top with a complacency shoulder that leads to a multi-week downtrend ending with a prolonged consolidation. If you observe social media channels during the top and bottom stages, you will see how precise the emotions are.

(Presenting the Bitcoin example again – during the 20k run at the end of 2017 you might have seen targets of 100k thrown around Twitter almost every 5 minutes. It was an evident euphoria as we received text messages from people never interested in crypto, asking how to buy Bitcoin. A similar experience occurred on the way down – there were people publicly announcing their exit from crypto when altcoins were finishing their cycles and Bitcoin was hovering around 7000$. Needless to say, after a few of those confessions, the market recovered and the capitulation was officially done.)

This chart should be, of course, taken with a grain of salt as it is only a model that is not supposed to be studied precisely. It also has its origins way before Cryptocurrencies existed and since this market is much more dynamic, people often joke that this is how a proper market cycle should look like:

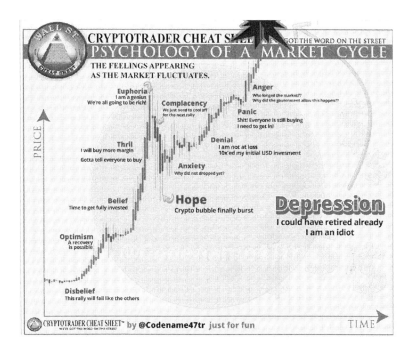

(The picture was taken from:
https://steemit.com/trade/@codename47/wallstreet-cheat-sheet-fixed-this-is-cryptotrader-s-cheat-sheet)

As much as that would be correct in a bull market, we, unfortunately, cannot experience only ups, as the cycles are a natural behaviour of an asset. No matter how strong the fundamentals might feel at the current moment or how much you believe TA does not work - you should never be caught up into the conviction that your coin is not subject to market cycles. Even if not precisely this one, there are a few other models which vary in their explanation, but the overall theory remains very similar.

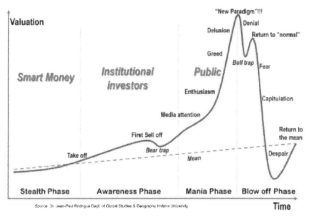

(The picture was taken from: http://blog.eckelberry.com/of-course-were-in-a-bubble-duh/)

(This one represents more the overview of the cycle with the background included. Current projections (April 2018) varying from 20k to even 1 million by the likes of Tim Draper and John McAfee, would probably put Bitcoin at the First Sell off stage. That is, however, very speculative although we would like to believe that with the upcoming adoption, we are yet to see the most significant growth this market has to offer.)

(The picture was taken from:
https://www.tradingacademy.com/lessons/article/psychological-ebbs-flows-markets/)

This example, on the other hand, while lacking a technical aspect, matches perfectly the emotions included in the other models. The brief explanation of the most important ones would go like this:

- Euphoria – a perfect spot to sell if anybody is able to catch it. A place where the sentiment is overly enthusiastic, and the price usually experiences parabolic growth.

- Complacency/Denial – with a lot of bullishness still left on the market, the sudden drop is very often faced with the denial (the fundamentals are so good, why would it fall now? It will recover shortly). This would serve as the perfect spot for an exit as well if the previous stage was not clear enough.

- Panic/Capitulation – the worst place to sell if you did not do it before. This is a stage where price accelerates going down and usually ends with a big capitulation wick. Selling during those stages has a high risk of getting rid of your position at basically the bottom.

- Disbelief/Dismay – this is when you should accumulate your favourite coins. It comes after the price stabilises from the accelerated selling and starts going sideways. This period can take weeks or even months, so there is no rush to market buy your positions here. The start of the uptrend here is very often met with disbelief as investors are still sore from the previous downtrend (this is another short run, no way it is sustainable).

- Hope – the stage where you already want to have all your positions leading to the top. You sell parts of your positions in here and just enjoy the uptrend. This one ends in the first-mentioned euphoria, and that is how the whole market cycle plays out.

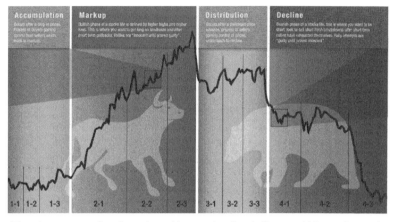

(The picture was taken from: http://www.visualcapitalist.com/this-market-cycle-diagram-explains-the-best-time-to-buy-stocks/)

(Last example of another model that confirms the previous theories. There is a slight difference here with complacency shoulder being labelled as the distribution, which in our opinion is more accurate. Price usually does not go straight down but rather gives time for smart money to exit their positions before the decline.)

The most important thing to understand about market cycles is that they are an unavoidable part of any coin in the market. Do not counter trade them at the top even if the fundamentals feel strong but also do not expect them to play out exactly as the models show. Not every time does the price have to come back to the previous accumulation zone nor does it always have to hit new ATH.

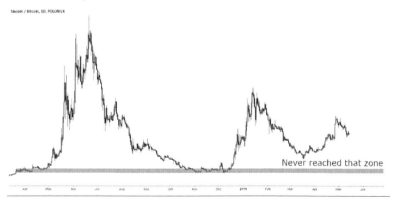

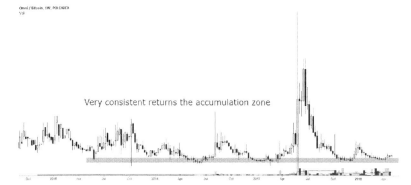

Very consistent returns the accumulation zone

They should serve as a tool to spot entries and exits in your mid to long-term positions and should always be confirmed by other indicators. We will talk more about those later on in this chapter, but right now we would like to explain trading strategies in both bull and bear markets briefly.

Bull vs Bear market

There is no excuse for a trader to make profits only in a bull market. The majority of people in Cryptocurrencies make good gains when altcoins and Bitcoin are running, only to lose 70% of their portfolio once the bear kicks in. The fact is, that if played correctly, a bear market can be almost as profitable as the bull, very often with less effort as well.

We will divide this part by presenting an optimal strategy for both bull and bear:

Bull market

During a bull market, there are a lot more opportunities to make money as basically every part of the cryptosphere is active – altcoins, ICOs, leverage trading. The strategy here depends solely on the person, if somebody wants to keep trading swings on Bitcoin or if they want to invest in alts.

From our experience – unless you are playing with high leverage – the easiest way to outperform the market itself is to trade altcoins and ICOs. If the conditions are right (which means that Bitcoin is not declining) you are gaining both in BTC and USD value at a rate much higher than you would by just trading Bitcoin. As the buying pressure in the market is high, ICOs with a short lock-up period are usually bringing instant profits and altcoins themselves are capable of doing several hundred % of growth in a matter of weeks.

The one thing that is extremely important in the bull market is taking profits – we will talk about it later as well because this is crucial. Too many people waste their bull market profits as they are afraid of missing out on even more of them in case they sell too early. Due to this approach, they often end up with half of their portfolio wiped out because they held through the distribution phase of the market cycle we discussed. Profits do not count until you sell and unless you understand that, you will have a hard time during the bear market.

We would also recommend staying away from the ICOs with a very long lock-up period, as there is a high chance they will be released during a bear market. That usually ends with them dropping to even 80% below the initial price, which is a loss in addition to opportunity cost. But other than that – feel free to trade with whatever you like as long as you are prepared for the potential declines on the market.

Bear market

Trading in a bear market is a lot more boring, and it usually comes down to how well you prepared during the bull. There are two main ways you could play it out – either by staying on the sidelines with your fiat or by actually trading it. We will focus on the latter.

Trading in a bear market basically means shorting, both Bitcoin and altcoins (more on this in the Margin Trading section). You can do that on a couple of exchanges (Bitfinex or Bitmex), and that should be your sole focus. At this point, if you prepared yourself correctly, you will not hold any significant altcoin positions as they will keep declining in value. You also probably do not want to participate in any ICOs as the buying pressure is extremely limited, and you are risking getting underwater with them. There are, however, some exceptions.

Even during the bear market, there are always some coins that do stand out and are not as affected by the Bitcoin drop as others. Usually, they perform well with the BTC pairing, often leaving them at breakeven USD-wise (as Bitcoin declines) but some coins outperform the decline as well.

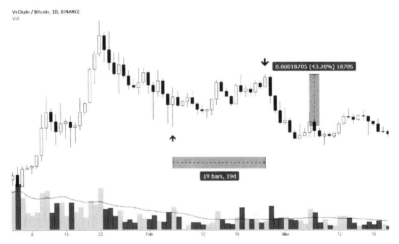

(VeChain was one of the coins that performed relatively well during the worst part of the February Bitcoin decline. Over the course of 19 days, it gained over 40% while the rest of the market dropped significantly, often to ATL in the case of newly released coins.)

As for the ICOs, there are some good opportunities as well, but those often depend on whether you manage to get into the presale (with better metrics than for regular investors). You should always focus on the ICOs with a low-cap that you are sure will sell out and create hype upon listing. Otherwise, the market conditions create too much fear to lure people into spending their money on crowd sales.

But since we said shorting is the primary way of trading during the bear market, let us continue. During the bull market, the portfolio is diversified into many different segments – alts, ICOs etc. During bear market, the portfolio should consist mostly of fiat or BTC if you are planning on trading. If that is the case, then you have almost all your investment resources focused on one thing (a little bit like going all-in a single alt). This, however, is a lot less risky since the potential loss is significantly lower with Bitcoin than in any alt.

From that moment on, it is all about trading the trend, which is bearish until proven otherwise. As you have seen, the altcoin markets can make a significant retracement from their tops due to cycles, and there is no exception with that on Bitcoin and any other large currency. This does not even require trading small swings – if we focus on a higher time frame, catching a good position near the top could bring a profit of few multipliers on an entire portfolio while just sitting back and watching it roll out. It works the same as you would trade an altcoin – remove some profits from the short on the way down and do not be stubborn to call the reversal.

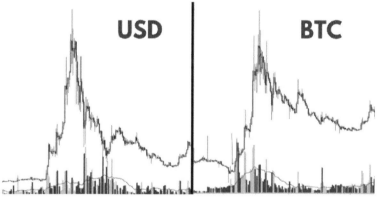

(USD and BTC charts of Ripple, one of the biggest currencies on the market. Even coins that big go through market cycles and are an excellent opportunity to short during a bear market.)

A bear market without a doubt requires more skills than the bull market as the TA proficiency is essential. However, if you learnt it well enough to feel comfortable while trading any altcoins swings (on lower time frames like 4H), a bear market can reward you a lot more than just staying on the sidelines would. Just be aware of the high market manipulation as that affects Bitcoin as well.

So, now that we know what our possibilities are let's dive into that legendary Alt season that everybody seems to be talking about.

Alt season

Before we begin we need to make one thing clear – Bitcoin was and still is the leading indicator for the whole market. Until altcoins get more FIAT pairs, they remain strictly correlated with Bitcoin as that is how they are evaluated. There are no strict rules on whether they grow only with Bitcoin going sideways or down, that is too inconsistent to be proven with certainty. They do, however, need stable market conditions as uncertainty in Bitcoin affects the whole market as well.

If we were to define an alt season, we would probably say that it is a period when it is a lot easier to win than lose. In a full swing season, you could literally choose a random coin on the big exchange that did not yet experience a pump and be almost certain of 100% gains in short to mid-term. It is both irrational and satisfying as well as rewarding and dangerous at the same time if not played correctly. Let us explain why.

(This is a weekly chart of Digibyte which pumped over 2200% in less than three weeks. Even if we are not counting catching the top, it is still a ridiculous 1700%, which believe it or not was held by a lot of people on the way down (which equals a loss of 95%).)

The chart presented above is the perfect example of how exponential the growth can get in Cryptocurrencies. If you have a strategy in place (and hopefully after you read this book, you will), this is everything a trader dreams about – high volatility with big up moves, very TA-friendly as it follows it with precision. However, if you are starting, more often than not you will be a part of that big black candle on the other side of the pump (one of us was very close to being that person as a matter of fact).

Alt season is a period where people's lives are changed in a matter of weeks, as it often takes one good trade to multiply your investment by 5/10/20 or even 100 times. Huge moves like these are the primary source of FOMO in traders. It is extremely hard to resist an ongoing pump especially if your coin did not move for the past couple of days when everybody else is winning. That is what makes the alt season hard for beginners – sticking to your picks and not falling for other traders promoting their bags.

With so many coins on the market and everything seeing exponential growth, it is very easy to get lost and abandon your current strategy. We are constantly seeing people jumping from one position to the other, catching 20/30% gains while their initial position would have been an easy 200% if they stayed with it. The name of the game in alt season is patience and overtrading is limiting your upside. To reduce the FOMO, you should understand a few things:

- You cannot catch all the pumps. There are several thousand coins on the market, and the majority of the good ones will experience a good pump. Catching all of them is neither possible nor profitable as you would over-diversify your portfolio.

- Traders exaggerate their success. Seeing others claiming they are constantly cashing out x3/4/5 gains is not a true representation of their skills. They never mention those coins that did not move or even lost value so do not get caught up in the bragging (everybody has those gains in a bull market).

- It is all speculation. Your goal is to make profits, not to stay attached to your investment. If you feel like you missed out on a great project, you will have another chance to get into it (go back to market cycles chapter). In the meantime, try making the same amount of money on other coins, even if you do not like them as much.

Having a rational approach to the market is essential. Being biased towards some projects will prevent you from looking into better opportunities out there, and the end goal is still the same – to make a profit. There are also several common rules that repeat themselves during the alt season. They could be presented as follows:

- Coins from the same "market" often run together

(When one "weed" coin pumps, all the other ones usually follow. Same happens with every new trend – if a big privacy coin like Monero pumps, you could expect the smaller ones to follow as well.)

- Pumps usually start with big caps and then proceed to the smaller ones

(With every alt season there is at least one big high cap coin that reaches irrational heights – not long ago it was done by Cardano and very recently (April 2018) it was EOS which reached 17 billion dollars valuation while only having a test-net.)

- Being "overbought" is a myth

(Coins can sustain irrational growth way longer than you would expect. We would not advise swinging the trades only because their RSI shows them being extended. We cannot count how many big pumps we missed because we thought it was the top. Alt season makes you question that again and again.)

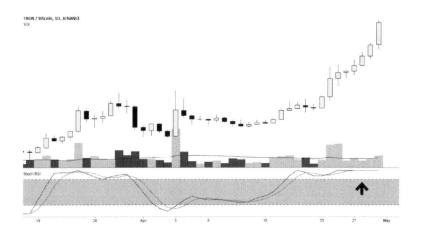

- Microcaps are a different market

(Tiny coins (below 5 million in market cap or on tiny exchanges) do not react the same way as other altcoins. They can be more stable during market crashing and often tend to run even when the market conditions are not bullish. Treat those tiny caps as an entirely different market that can be played during any period, bullish or bearish.)

- Altcoins outperform Bitcoin

(Very often people sell their altcoins when Bitcoin starts moving up – do not do this. Those altcoins dips that appear when BTC is running are usually small and tend to recover very quickly. Unless you predict your coin will hit a prolonged downtrend, it is always better to appreciate in both BTC and USD values. Staying in Bitcoin while the whole market is pumping is the missed opportunity even if Bitcoin's price is increasing as well. If you sell your coin to catch Bitcoin's pump, you can be almost sure you will have to repurchase it higher. Keep in mind this applies only to alt season, holding alts is not a recommended strategy for all market periods.)

Fine, but you might ask – how do I know that the alt season is coming? The answer to that could be either found in individual charts (where most are back to their accumulation zones) or by looking at the percentage of Total Market Cap.

One of the best indicators of the alt season is threatening Bitcoin's dominance. From the beginning of 2017, all the major altcoin movements appeared when the rest of the market started stealing away that dominance. It does not mean that Bitcoin was declining as well, it just stayed sideways while the alts kept on increasing in value, therefore taking more significant shares of the market. In general, you should not associate losing dominance with losing value – there were several occasions where altcoins were growing alongside Bitcoin and still managed to increase their percentage in the total market cap.

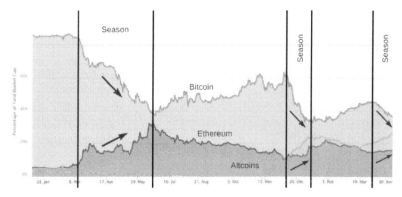

(Very often Ethereum is known as the top indicator for alt season to start, and while there is some truth to it, it is not necessarily always the case. The chart above presents the percentage of Total Market Cap from the beginning of 2017, and as you can see, each decline in Bitcoin dominance significantly resulted in alts gaining. Ethereum is not always the part of it as you can see in March when alts rallied against the dominant trend.)

Based on that dominance indicator and the overall alt market being back at their high time frame bottoms it is rational to expect a small rally soon. Whether it transforms into a full-blown alt season or ends prematurely depends on the market conditions.

(The run in December 2017 ended quickly because Bitcoin entered a major downtrend which caused panic. The previous one in summer 2017 lasted a lot longer as there was no reason for the market to slow down as it was in the middle of the biggest popularity boom it has ever been (which started a run from 20 billion to over 800 in 10 months).)

Nothing is certain when it comes to crypto. There is a chance we might never see May-June 2017 alt market again, and there is a chance we might be on the verge of one, exactly one year later. Whatever the market is going to decide, it is essential never to get lost in it and approach trading calmly. And that is why we will discuss trading psychology.

Trading psychology

Having proficiency in TA or good instincts in FA means nothing if you cannot control emotions while trading. Not selling the coin after the clear blow-off top because of greed is only one of the examples why trading psychology is so critical. It is not just about controlling the emotions – it is also about using them to your advantage.

An essential skill to have is to understand how to react to your own emotions. We highly recommend having a trading diary – a notebook where you write down all your emotions while trading. Figure out how you behave when the market is dumping and which emotions you experience when you have a profit. Those feelings, as you have seen with market cycles, are just as good indicators as TA.

(It is not a coincidence when people often say that their coin starts pumping a second after they sold it. Feeling of capitulation is probably one of the best indicators of the bottom being close. Buy the fear, sell the greed – there are not many trading tips so useful as this one, but even those extreme emotions often need practice before you can recognise them while trading.)

When you are not experienced enough to be capable of controlling your emotions entirely even during the biggest pumps, you need a system that would do it for you. The system should suit your character and availability of time – do not day trade if you are very busy and cannot handle a lot of stress. If you want to have more time for other things and only do few trades per week, choose to invest instead.

Having a system in place eliminates all the mistakes that you would have done if you were making your trades "on-the-go". It helps you to:

- Fight off fear – whether it is fear of missing out or fear of buying when the market is panicking, a good set of rules can solve both issues. This is probably the most common emotion that traders battle with and it is easily countered with previously set buy orders and precise rules on entering the coin.

- Fight off greed – the main reason why new traders cannot sustain their profits. Again, a precise system of taking profits allows the traders to secure not only them but also asses bigger pumps much more calmly than usual.

- Keep consistency – sometimes when confidence in your own trades decreases, the profitability does as well. Sticking to the strategy guarantees a quick recovery after a series of bad trades.

Up to this point you should already know how to do your research, read/create charts and understand how the market cycles play out. From this point on, we can proceed to the actual trading process.

Setting up a trading strategy

Once you have evaluated how much time you can spend on crypto, it is finally time to start setting up your strategy. For those that have not yet decided which playing style would fit them best, we prepared a summary that showcases all the major pros and cons.

Trading vs HODLing

Day trading

Probably the most stressful and demanding style of playing. It requires good TA skills and a lot of free time but is the most rewarding in the short-term. Day trading is basically doing several small trades (5-15%) per day on micro moves on high liquidity coins (only major alts in the top 20 or Bitcoin can provide that).

Pros	Cons
• Quick profits • Does not necessarily require FA knowledge • Does not require attention apart from trading hours	• Demands good TA skills • Can be stressful • Time-consuming • Impossible to do on smaller coins • If not leveraged – requires bigger trading capital

This strategy is mostly recommended for people with bigger capital and sharp skills, since, if played correctly, it can be very profitable. For a new trader, the amount of stress and time needed to control the set-ups might be a bit overwhelming.

Swing trading

An extended version of day trading, where the set-ups last several days to even over a week depending on the opportunity. Swing trading usually means riding the uptrends leading to a significant event and quickly reinvesting the profits into the next short-term trade. This is often an excellent complementary strategy to long-term investments as sometimes those short trades can be as profitable as multi-week holdings.

Pros	Cons
• Very profitable and requires less time than day trading • Allows to keep high portfolio flexibility • Can be played on lower caps as well • Enable the trade to play-out and potentially become a long-term hold, instead of cutting it early	• Requires experience in TA as entries are more dynamic • Higher risk as price action is usually outside of bigger time frame bottom • Proper portfolio management is a must since the asset allocation changes a lot

This is probably the most flexible style of trading, as it includes both quick profits and building a strong long-term position if the growth turns out stronger than expected. It requires both FA and TA to master the swings fully.

Investing

The other name to it would be a cycle trader – a person that invests on the bottom and holds through the whole market cycle, selling on the way up and near the top. It is a strategy that allows the trader to maintain a very good work-life balance as most of the work is done during the accumulation period. After that, the only action the investor takes is cashing out the profits and reinvesting them in the positions that have not pumped yet. This is our primary trading style.

Pros	Cons
• Doesn't require much attention • Allows to maximise the gains by waiting until the top signal appears • Fairly easy to trade as accumulation period usually lasts weeks • By taking profits on the way up, it maintains the portfolio's liquidity	• No way to predict if the coin is going to underperform • Compared to shorter trades, this one is highly correlated with overall market condition (must be good) • Requires strong profit-taking strategy

We would recommend having few investments in every portfolio, even if your main playing strategy is day trading.

No matter how good you are, these are the trades that often change lives as they can go over 20x during the period of a single market cycle. It does not require much time to be updated on the coin, but it is gratifying if proper research is done before.

HODLing

As HODL became a running joke in the cryptosphere, there is a big group of people that believe in very long-term holding. The point of HODLing is not to sell the coins even after experiencing massive gains, with a looming downtrend. We do not believe this is a viable strategy because of the frequent market cycles that every coin goes through. It is a significant opportunity cost that cripples the trader's flexibility and points at their inability to react to the market's behaviour.

Pros	Cons
<ul><li>Requires no supervision</li><li>No TA skills are necessary</li><li>If fundamentals are strong – the results can be very rewarding</li></ul>	<ul><li>Huge opportunity cost</li><li>Limits portfolio's flexibility</li><li>No guarantee of the coin ever recovering to the previous levels after the dump</li></ul>

Taking a trade obviously requires either TA or FA skills (usually both), but there is often a question which one should be favoured more. Apart from the extreme cases (day trading and HODLing), it is essential to know how to create a balance between these two; therefore, we would like to discuss how to utilise both FA and TA.

FA vs TA

One of the old time classic questions in all trading – which one is more reliable, TA or FA? In our opinion – a mixture of both.

The Cryptocurrency market is very easily manipulated (we will be talking about this in the last chapter), therefore news often have a more significant impact on the price than they would on other markets. TA still very often predicts the movements and aligns with FA when they appear, but the probability of few people controlling a particular coin's supply is too big to trust TA completely.

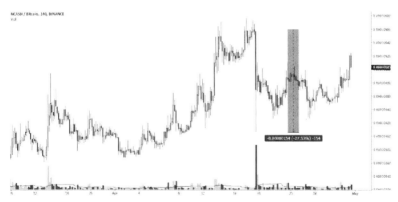

(A strong move up that got halted because of FUD circulating nCash, resulted in an instant -27% drop. This is why you should always be aware of what is happening with the project as those random events cannot be predicted solely by TA.)

There is a lot of flexibility when it comes to deciding on how you want to trade, meaning that the edge can be given to either FA or TA. It is even possible, but that equals to being exposed to much more significant risk, that is why we recommend always to have a mixture of both:

- When focusing on TA, use FA to find out if there are any risks associated with the project (developer disappearing, scam reports) and if there any catalysts for a possible jump (launch of a platform, new website).

- When focusing on FA, use TA to find proper entries near the support and set yourself exits according to resistance.

Relying solely on one of them will expose you to the risk of an inevitable crush either due to lousy entry far from support or market event that could have been predicted with proper research. It is also good to have in mind both FA and TA in case one of them needs to be counter traded.

(With a coin finishing its market cycle even the best news usually see a quick full retracement. That happened with Stellar when the currency announced the partnership with IBM. The price saw a massive spike of around 200% only to drop to previous levels and start consolidating before the real uptrend began again. If a person would go only by FA and ignored the role of TA/market cycles they would probably stay underwater for days or weeks before being profitable.)

(This works the other way as well, as it was visible during the recent (April 2018) Bitcoin downtrend. Majority of traders were predicting a sudden drop due to 2014 fractal even when fundamentals suggested otherwise (reports of big players wanting to buy into the market, bullish sentiment appearing, positive press about Bitcoin from around the world). Finally, the Bitcoin jumped to over 9000 in the next couple of days, leaving a lot of people on the sidelines. If a person would go only by TA here and ignored the role of FA, they would be left out of a very significant market recovery which saw the total capitalisation grow more than 150 billion dollars.)

Taking a trade

We finally arrived to probably the most crucial part of this book. No aspect is more important in a trade than a good entry, and not many things cause as many problems as selling. In this chapter, we will go through finding the best setups for taking a trade and exiting it. In order to avoid repeating previous theory, we will be using a lot of terms and knowledge from the earlier chapters so make sure you have read through them as well.

Finding entries and accumulating

Having a proper entry is essential not only because it allows you to maximise gains, but also to minimise the chances of getting underwater. The definition of a good position depends on what time frame we are looking at for that specific trade. From a short-term perspective, we are turning to TA for a right spot, while long-term trades should be confirmed by FA a well.

While reading the following methods, keep in mind that nobody catches an exact bottom and sells the absolute top. Do not try to be perfect as you might miss out on a good position and always take people who brag about selling the top with a grain of salt. Once you got this, here is how to find a good entry:

Short-term

- Buy on strong horizontal supports or the base of a bullish pattern. This basically means entering the trade wherever you would expect a bounce from the price before it is ready to move further. We explained optimal entries in the TA chapter with patterns, Ichimoku Cloud, Bollinger Bands or EMAs, so if you do not remember them, please go back to those segments. The entries should be approved with some other indicators (low volume of the dump, bullish divergences) and with a tight stop-losses set just below that support (more on stop-losses later in this chapter).

- Buy the rumour. We will explain trading market events in the latter part of this chapter, so in this section, we will briefly describe the general concept. When there is an important upcoming event (exchange/partnership announcement), the price tends to react positively to it. There is usually a larger spike at the start of the rumour, and the uptrend continues until the real announcement is made. This serves as an excellent opportunity for a short-term swing if you can manage to get a respectable entry, despite the hype slowly being priced-in.

- Buy the FUD. Cryptocurrencies are still a very young industry, as the companies taking part often have problems with fulfilling investor's expectations. Due to that, there are often misunderstandings that can get overblown very quickly, having an almost instant negative effect on the price. Depending on how serious the concerns are, this often serves as a great buying opportunity. In many cases, those reports and people complaining are just exaggerating facts and do not have any substance in them. That does not, however, stop people from selling their positions, so if you can confirm that this is nothing but a FUD, you are looking at the rapid gains opportunity.

(Example of that might be a small cap Haven, which was accused of being a pump&dump coin because a group of popular profiles tried to control its price. The attempts were unsuccessful, and they never managed to enter the coin, but since the project was now associated with scammers, it significantly dropped in the following days. Nothing fundamental changed about the currency itself, that is why despite the bad reputation, it recovered, rewarding people that bought the dip.)

Long-term

- From a long-term perspective, the best buys are made on a high time frame bottoms after the retracement from the previous market cycle. The purchases should be made after the capitulation is visible (accelerated selling) and when the price stops making lower lows. This is a so-called accumulation zone, where regular people lose patience and sell their positions for a loss while smart money buys in for the upcoming uptrends.

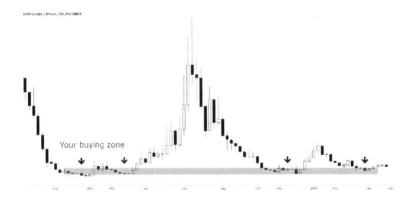

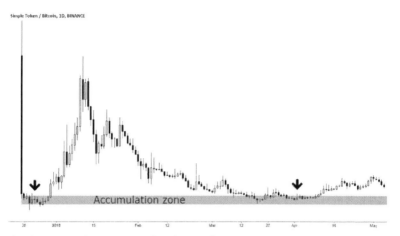

(Prices tend to come back to their previous accumulation zones. Very often they are so accurate that you can set a buy order a few months earlier and still basically nail the perfect entry.

For further confirmation, use the volume profiles and sometimes popular reversal patterns – in November/December 2017 the majority of alts signalled the end of the downtrend by making double bottom Adam & Eve patterns.)

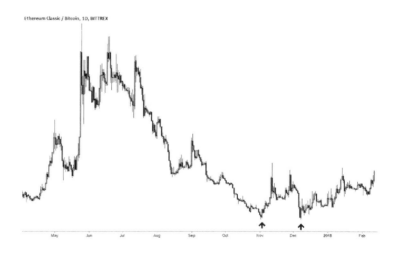

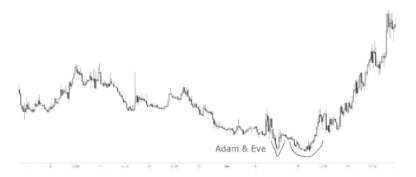

Since Cryptocurrencies are very volatile, there are situations where the price does not retrace to the absolute bottom, but quickly reverses with very little or no consolidation at all. If you do not want to wait for the confirmation of the uptrend, you should be looking to enter at the top of the nearest strong horizontal support as shown in the examples below:

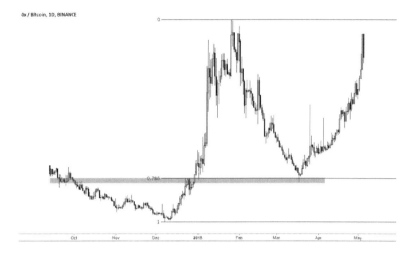

- Obviously, you want to buy when the fundamentals are strong (whole chapter one). The project must be proven to be able to deliver, and its roadmap should point at having a lot of catalysts in the new future that can spark uptrends. No matter how good the entry from TA perspective is, you need to have strong fundamentals if you plan on investing long-term.

- Buy when nobody is talking about it. The difference between 2x and 10x depends on whether you bought it once you "heard" of it or actually "found" it. As we talked before, the exposure is what gets the price moving, and there is no better place to enter when there is lack of it. Finding such coins requires a lot of research but it is very gratifying. Do not settle for those small opportunities that hard-working people already benefited from when they found them first. Spend time looking for those hidden gems as that is one of the main ways of outperforming the market.

- According to the market cycles' emotions, the best buys are made during anger and depression stages. For us, the best indicator of that is when we post a tweet about buying altcoins, and we receive dozens of messages that this is a terrible idea per "altcoins are dead". This, of course, needs to be supported by TA as the same things can be heard just before capitulation. However, if the emotional pattern matches price consolidation, there is a high chance that you are entering the price at the bottom.

Since we used the term accumulation here, we should very briefly explain what it means. Accumulation is, in other words, a process of building a position within a certain period (until we are happy with our bags). A rule that you should always use when buying either short or long-term – always try to set bids instead of market buying. When you are accumulating a coin that low, even few % in price can make a huge difference for the future pump. Because of that, always try to set bids at the lower parts of the consolidation zone and be patient with them getting filled.

Do not mistake accumulation with averaging down – averaging down is the process of increasing your position once it fell from your initial buying zone. It is done to get a better average buying price, and it is a viable strategy if the dip was not a signal for a further downtrend. This, however, should only be done if the initial buy was at strong support as well – a lot of people average down from the absolute top to the bottom, while this strategy should only be used if the initial setup failed.

Finding exits and taking profits

You can never be sure about what is going to happen on the market. Cryptocurrencies are incredibly volatile, and every small piece of news has a strong influence on the prices. Being greedy is the main reason why so many people are experiencing loss despite crypto being called the easiest market out there. Those people were hesitant to have a profit-taking strategy, very often because of the fear of losing additional gains. In this chapter, we would like to teach you how to be able to finally hit that sell button, a process, so many people struggle with.

How do I sell my position?

There are few ways that traders can exit their positions – some do it once at the top, some do it partially. From our experience, the most logical way of doing it is setting a few targets and selling small amounts on the way up. This way, we not only still have position's right size going forward but also secure profits in case of a crash. This way we have free money to play other coins, which often have high risk/reward ratio since they are still unpumped.

Taking profits both for short and long-term looks very similar, as only the time frame of the trade changes. Therefore, we will be explaining them without the distinction of the trade's duration.

How much % should I sell each time?

The size of the sell should depend on your confidence in the project and the chart's potential. If your coin has solid fundamentals and chart points at even potential x10, do not sell half of your position on the first resistance. During an average trade, we would be selling from 10 to 20% at each stop, but this is not a universal rule. With some projects, we will sell 50%, and with others, we will not do anything until it reaches 3rd or 4th resistance. It is up to you to decide how exposed to the risk you want to be. Whatever your strategy turns out to be, remember to follow this set of rules:

- Set your sells according to the market condition. If the market is bullish let the coins run longer than usual, they might try reaching their ATHs. If the market is bearish, do not fall in love with your currency – cut most it whenever you have made a profit on it. You have to be flexible and reactive to the conditions, as there is no one way of playing the market.

- No matter how much you believe in the project, do not be afraid to sell it. It is subject to market cycles as well so you can be sure it will not go up forever.

- Always zoom out to decide how much potential you still have. When you are close to the parabolic blow-off top, do not be hesitant to release most of your position at once.

- Leave yourself a "moon bag". When exiting a position, do not sell everything. Leave about 10-15% left in case the coin decides to go even higher (unless it was a definite top) so that you can still gain from that move and not feel FOMO in case you miss it.

How do I set those targets?

Setting those targets depends on what kind of coin we are dealing with. If this is a project with rich price history, it is more comfortable as we would just set our targets at the most crucial resistance zones (just like with entries, we suggest going back to the TA chapter to see how different indicators can help in determining perfect selling spots). If the coin has little price history and breaching ATH is very possible, we usually use fib extensions to assess our next targets.

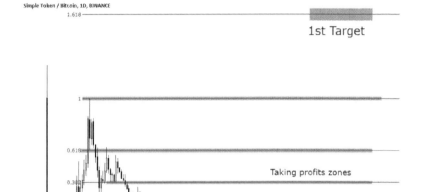

However, if the coin is new and it has no previous price history, the targets get a little bit trickier. In cases like this, we could set some psychological targets, but most of the time it still comes down to observing the price action.

(Psychological resistances do not really qualify as regular targets, but this allows you to leave the trade running to some extent. If a coin is worth 10 cents, those resistances can appear at every other significant price – 20 cents, 50 cents, 1 dollar etc. Never base your profit on a taking strategy, as this is only a supportive method in sporadic cases.)

Also, do not be afraid to set very high targets - even if you do not hit them, it is always worth a shot as many coins have thin order books that might get triggered by a big buy. Same goes the other way for buy orders – having low bids sometimes results in catching capitulation wicks which we discussed in the previous chapter.

Are these targets enough?

In both cases – with and without price history – some constant observation is recommended. With so many unexpected events you might miss out on a lot if the trade was left running for weeks. Positions should be evaluated on the go to see if there are no other bearish signals that might point at taking the profits earlier (key resistance/fib, bearish divergences, a bearish pattern like rising wedges, blow-off top). Whenever you are late in taking profits before an unexpected dump appeared, make sure you do not panic. Each drop is followed by a small bounce which should serve as your selling spot if you are not confident in a coin's recovery.

Alongside TA you should also look at the emotions surrounding your specific coin. If the atmosphere around it seems too euphoric (calling it the next bitcoin), reevaluate your position as this might be the time to sell. The drops from the top are usually the most brutal; therefore, we would suggest sticking to the rule we mentioned previously – buy the fear, sell the greed (go back to the market sentiment part of the first chapter).

Those are the rules that should be enough for you to create your own profit-taking strategy. Do it on the way up, judge the proportions based on the potential left and do not be afraid to sell almost everything when the top is near. It will probably take some time for you to figure out what levels best fit with your risk tolerance but the important part is that you will be taking those profits in the first place. This alone puts you over most traders and opens other opportunities for you as you continue to have free funds.

The last part of this chapter, before we get to the portfolio management, focuses on market events. Without further ado, let us explain what "buy the rumour, sell the news" means.

Trading market events

Cryptocurrencies, due to the nature of the technology, have a set of few events that are very common and are often seen as excellent investment opportunities. We mostly have in mind forks and airdrops, but since we are talking about market events, we think it is wise to talk about trading them in general.

We differentiate two main types of events that often confuse people about how they should be played – previously mentioned fork/airdrop and in addition to that – exchange listing. Before we talk about them, we should look at how, in theory, every market event should be played out.

General Announcements

The first and only rule that you should be following here is „Buy the rumour, sell the news". It does not even need to apply to trading based on rumours directly – it is just a reminder to sell the asset just before the hype hits its peak. Depending on the type of the announcement, the run-up to the event should serve as an excellent short-term trade if you manage to exit before the majority decides to do it as well. This, however, only applies to the announcement that might potentially hold a lot of value – revealing a partnership, product release, exchange listing, coin burn. If the event does not keep a lot of importance, the price is usually already fully priced-in, and the chances of it having a further impact are small.

(Examples of non-important events include a release of the roadmap, conference speeches (unless it's a major conference) or a new website reveal. This, however, might not apply to very low cap coins, as at early stages of their development, even small milestones might be significant. That is because it allows them to reach a bigger audience once promoted.)

The moment of selling should be timed not just before the announcement is done but a bit earlier – if everybody wants to sell it before, you need to act against them as well. As usual, we would suggest taking the profits on the way up so that even if your dump comes earlier, you still secure some of the money. Time frame here would be ranging from a day to a couple of days before the announcement as a right spot to sell the position.

And now, moving on to the more specific ones with examples so that you can have a better understanding of the topic:

Exchange listing

A brief note before we start explaining – no coin is allowed to disclose being listed on a top exchange (Binance, Bittrex), therefore if the coin announces future listings – it probably means other platforms.

Playing exchange listing is tricky because it involves not only picking a right moment to sell but also a right moment to buy (if we are not in already). For us to explain it, we need to assume that our coin is going from a smaller exchange (let's say KuCoin) to a big one (for example Binance) in a sudden announcement (without previous rumours and signals about it). Most of the time this scenario goes like this:

- A big initial pump on the existing exchange

- Retracement

- A volatile action once trading is active on the new exchange – usually a very high first buy, followed by small uptrend and a prolonged retracement afterwards.

- Once the price settles – coin experiences a stable continuation

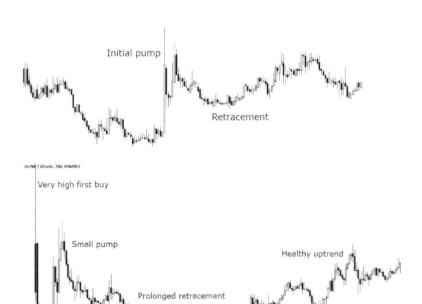

The perfect strategy for a person who wants maximise profits would be to sell the coins on the primary pump on the existing exchange/new one, and then buy in on the bottom of the retracement after the action settles. Selling at those levels, however, is very hard as the volatility often makes the prices jump 100% only to retrace in a matter of minutes fully. You should never jump in right after the coin is listed, as the significant volume is not sustainable and the price always needs to find its support first. HODLers in this situation usually tend to stay on the sidelines as the new exchanges bring additional value anyway, despite the short-term volatility.

Additionally, two other scenarios are worth mentioning here briefly, as they give you the full perspective on playing the exchange listings:

- There is an announcement days/week before the listing – play this as you would in any other event as explained before. Right before the announcement, either set tight stop-losses or take profits. Best case scenario, you will be selling the top with a possibility of entering lower. Worst case scenario, you will lose out on some additional profit, but the opportunity to enter will appear once again. As we mentioned before, no significant exchange can be announced by the coin beforehand; therefore, the spike in price is not expected to be that significant.

- The currency is already on a significant exchange/a new one is a low-tier exchange – these cases when a new exchange does not bring a lot of value to the coin are basically non-events. They cause a small spike in price, but the risk/reward ratio here is not worth the action. Unless you want to risk losing your good entry for a couple of %, we would recommend not playing the listing.

Airdrop

By an airdrop we mean the distribution of free coins either among the investors of a particular asset (usually by the rate of 1:1, but that may differ) or among people registered for the launch of the new coin.

For projects that start as an airdrop (at the end of the book we list a source where you can find them) the strategy is as simple as HODLing. Usually, after the coins are distributed, the first few weeks are met with enormous selling pressure, making it hard to sustain any value. After that, when the price stabilises, the coins are left only in the hands of confident investors and begin their usual uptrends.

Since you receive the coins for free, there is no reason why you should be actively trading them right after the airdrop. The scenario explained above is how it usually plays out, but often, it is tough to catch the moment of reversal; therefore, we would suggest simply holding the position. The registration process is quick, and even those small amounts that are sent can turn out to be a good source of income if done regularly. The situation, however, looks completely different if it is an established coin that does the airdrop to its holders.

An announcement that it will reward its holders with free coins at the specific date is one of the most hype-building events you can meet in the whole crypto. Those are usually the biggest gainers during the alt season, especially if the airdropped coins also have a significant value.

(One of the best examples of how significant an airdrop can be for the coin's value is the drop of Ignis tokens on NXT. The price during 35 days went, depending on the entry, from 1500% to even 1800%. The Ignis was a solid project that was supposed to bring a lot of value to the ecosystem as well. Unfortunately, because the first investors were looking only for quick profit, it kept declining for the next four months. The same thing happened with NXT which had its market cycle downtrend accelerated to a great extent as most of the investors were inside of it solely for the airdrop.)

Playing the airdrop usually depends on the quality of the receiving coin. When the airdropped currency is strong, the most profitable way is following the General Announcements strategy. That way we do not only sell at the peak of the pump, but we can also buy the airdropped tokens cheap, shortly after the investors dump them. Some people prefer to play it 50/50 (sell 50% and hold the rest for the airdrop), but that has a high risk of not selling the airdrop quickly enough to outperform selling the original coin.

When the airdrop quality is less significant, the whole event also plays a less significant role in the coin's price action. It may, of course, cause accelerated growth and result in a small retracement after the pump, but usually, for investors, this is not something even worth swinging. When you look at

the airdrop, make sure you evaluate the importance of it –
drops are happening at least a few times a week for various
coins, and most people do not realise it. If you do, however,
spot a strong one – make sure not to sell it too early, as the
run has the potential to go parabolic if the market conditions
are favourable.

Fork

In this category, we would like to focus on a situation, when
the altcoin proceeds to create a completely new coin, at the
same time abandoning or changing the structure of the
original one. We can discuss these examples on one currency
called ZClassic. During the last year, two significant forks
were coming from it – ZenCash and Bitcoin Private.

ZenCash was the fork coming from an already established
ZClassic coin with an active development team. It was
supposed to bring new value to Crypto as a completely
anonymous currency, and as of today (April 2018), it hovers
around 150M in the market cap. The team promised to keep
the original coin ZClassic supported even after the fork, but
that did not change the outcome of the trade as it still
crashed.

(The price of ZClassic during ZenCash events. After the announcement and leading to the fork itself, it gained over 1600% in BTC value alone. The moment after the fork was done, the price fully retraced, at one moment even hitting the absolute price bottom, crashing the coin completely.)

ZenCash showed a lot of potential, a lot more than ZClassic could offer. Many people were willing to hold it as they got to keep both the original coin and a new promising one. There is, however, no force on the market that could have stopped people from selling ZCL as its main purpose at that time was basically to provide people with free ZEN.

In cases where the fork looks to be valuable, it might be worth holding part of the position (the bigger it is, the more risk you are taking) through the fork to sell it directly after the listing. The original coin, of course, should be sold before the fork and directly after, so do not ever look at its fundamentals because it will not matter – the coin will crash a second after the event is done. Keep in mind that this scenario is very rare as the upcoming fork should really stand out to be worth holding. Otherwise, it is a very big risk, that is why we would always recommend selling at least 50% of the initial coin before the event happens.

(In the end, ZenCash managed to almost instantly reach 16$, while ZCL at the peak was worth around 9$. If the sell orders were hit, a person would have gotten profit from holding and still would recover some money from selling the ZClassic. It was not an easy trade as the price was very volatile, but if it was played correctly, it was one of the better opportunities on the market at that time.)

Bitcoin Private, on the other hand, was the fork that appeared after abandoned ZClassic was picked up by a new development team. Here as well, we could have heard the promises of keeping the original coin supported, but this time nobody fell for the same trick twice.

(The price of ZClassic during the Bitcoin Private events. From the moment of the announcement to the top there was nearly 20000% increase in BTC value. The selling here started before the fork itself and accelerated heavily after it was done, resulting once again in full retracement. ZCL at the top was worth almost 200$ while Bitcoin Private at best during March-April 2018 was peaking at 80$ per coin.)

To sum up this chapter of playing market events – usually, the safest and most profitable way of dealing with events is to sell the main pump that was triggered by the announcement. Everything that comes after it, whether it is exchange listing, airdrop or fork, the price tends to take a deep dive due to people taking profits and their free coins. Staying for the event itself is extremely risky and should never be done unless there is a good reason behind it (which in this case would mean either high-quality airdrop or fork, but that is extremely rare).

Managing your portfolio

Being great at finding hidden gems and trading them does not mean much in the long-term perspective without proper portfolio management. Every investor should have a specific strategy on their coins are distributed and what percentage of overall portfolio can go into a single trade. This is different for every trader as everybody has a different risk tolerance and capital size, but some universal rules should be followed despite those differences.

Portfolio diversification

Building your portfolio depends on a few factors – the amount of capital, your risk tolerance and availability of time for trading. Depending on those, you will either create for yourself a portfolio with a couple of long-term holds or for example one dominated with BTC to day-trade alts. No matter what your goal is, these are the rules you should have in mind while constructing your portfolio:

Construct it around risk segments

Every portfolio should have a few categories that represent different risk levels – high-cap investments, low-cap gambles, long-term Bitcoin hold, etc. This might be hard for new traders as it requires a lot of management in such a volatile market. However, with more significant portfolios, it is necessary to minimise the risks, so at least try to create a guide according to which you will manage your coins' allocation.

(Example of a structure from one of the biggest traders in crypto - @CryptoCobain.)

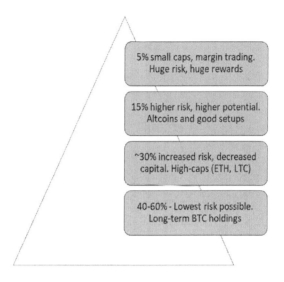

(This is a very rational structure, which we are using as well (with slight changes in percentages). The bigger the risk is, the smaller should be your overall capital invested in it. This might not be the most profitable setup, but it is the most logical from the risk management point of view. Take note that this structure is meant to represent general portfolio allocation – for a different market period such as alt season or bear market, it should be modified accordingly.)

Keep it within the structure

When you take profits from one of your positions, always try to keep the composition of the portfolio intact. Do not let one coin overtake the majority of it if you planned to have even distribution. This does not mean you should cut the position when it is pumping – it means that once it stops, you should distribute the profits according to your previously established levels. Sudden changes in the strategy can backfire as you are trading more spontaneously and therefore, more emotionally.

(When a low cap pumps 10x, take the profits and reinvest some of it to low-risk positions as well. Investing everything in more low caps will shift your portfolio into more risk-oriented one, significantly increasing its volatility. Unless you are prepared to see 5-10% swings on your overall portfolio regularly, we suggest distributing the profits on all categories.)

Do not over diversify

The more positions you have, the less exposed you are to the risk. However, too many coins also significantly limit your profitability, which means you should limit yourself to only a certain amount. If your capital is small, you want to maximise your potential gains with just a couple of positions. Big portfolios, on the other hand, aim for less volatility; therefore, a larger number of coins is justified. Keep in mind, however, that too many positions also make it difficult to keep up with their development on a day-to-day basis.

(From the experience, we can say ten coins are still manageable when it comes to being up-to-date with their progress. It is also a standard when it comes to the number of leading positions a regular trader holds. Sure, you can have over 100 coins like many famous traders do, but do not expect to outperform the market this way significantly.)

Never go all-in

Having too few positions exposes you to high risk, especially if you invest significant amounts. That is not only because of low liquidity (hard to quickly exit the position) but also because the volatility of the market can cut your portfolio by dozens of % in a matter of hours. Always try to protect yourself from unexpected market events that could crash your only position.

(As one of the biggest Cryptocurrency traders @needacoin preaches – if you have ten bags, you only need one of them to pump 10x to cover the losses of every other one going to

zero. *Having too many positions is not good but opening yourself up for a couple of them increases the chances of catching a winner that will cover your potential losers.)*

Always have some free BTC/ETH on the side

There is nothing worse for a trader than having no money to buy the dips. Instead of being stuck 100% in altcoins, you should always have some free BTC or ETH on the side to have more flexibility in your moves. This way you do not have to sell your positions to enter a quick opportunity that just appeared. This also keeps your portfolio stable as largest currencies are less volatile and are independent of other coins unlike all altcoins with only BTC/ETH trading pairs.

(The percentage of BTC/ETH in a portfolio depends on the market condition. During alt season being around 80/90% in alts is often a very profitable strategy as they are increasing in USD and BTC values. Apart from that period, however, we would recommend releasing many altcoins for BTC as whether it is running or dumping, you will lose a lot more by staying in them. If Bitcoin dumps, remember you can always open a short position.)

These rules should be able to guide you through creating your portfolio that would fit your playing style. Keep in mind that those are not strict guidelines – they present the most rational and risk-minimising approach that most traders are looking for. There are, however, successful traders that structure their portfolios in a completely different way. If you are focused mostly on mining micro caps or solely on investing into ICOs, you will have to restructure it according to your needs.

What is important to remember here is not to expose yourself to too much risk and always to maintain liquidity in your portfolio (not having a majority of portfolio stuck in coins that cannot be sold without crashing the market).

Risk management

Risk management is a popular phrase thrown around crypto-related threads, but it is very rarely explained or discussed. As the name suggests, it is a system of minimising the risks while trading, but what does it really mean? We will go through the most critical aspects of risk management in crypto by segments, as they are very diversified.

Stop-losses

Setting stop-losses in crypto is still an ongoing topic for discussion, as many traders believe that the trading environment makes them impossible to be used. We disagree with that statement, and we think stop-losses are an essential part of risk management.

The point of stop-loss is to prevent the investor from further losing money when the price is going down. It is set at a certain level so that when the price reaches it, it automatically sells the trader's position at a small loss. If triggered, it usually should not take more than a small percentage off the position, but that depends on the entry.

The main argument against stop-losses is that the market is too volatile and they get triggered too easily. Although we can agree with this statement as far as low liquidity coins are concerned, most of the time stop-losses do not work, because they are not used correctly. The right use of stop-losses is relatively simple, but it also requires another skill which causes a lot of problems – getting good entries.

Stop-loss should be set near the entry price but in a spot, that, if reached by price, would be the potential reversal or further dump signal. Spots like this, as you now know from the TA chapter, are below important support zones.

Having stop-losses set at these prices would not be possible if we had a worse entry. In that case, the potential losses are more significant as the stops should still be set under the support. In no case, you should ever set stop-losses based only on the percentage you are willing to lose. This method almost guarantees to get stopped-out as prices like to range between support and resistance, which you did not include in your setup. Here are few examples from our previous charts with included stop-losses:

On many exchanges, however, it is impossible to set stop-losses. In that case, we highly suggest setting up the alarms (in Blockfolio application as an example) to be able to react manually whenever the price reaches our point of interest. It is not very effective as the price often manages to fall already, but at least gives us the opportunity to sell on a recovery bounce.

Percent Loss Drawdown vs. Percent to Recover	
% Loss of Capital	% of Gain Required to Recoup Loss
10%	11.11%
20%	25%
30%	42.85%
40%	66.66%
50%	100%
60%	150%
70%	233%
80%	400%
90%	900%
100%	broke

(The picture was taken from: https://www.anirudhsethireport.com/why-risk-per-trade-is-so-important-percent-loss-drawdown-vs-percent-to-recover/)

(Proof of why it is so important to protect yourself from staying underwater. Many trades that fall over 90% in crypto never recover again.)

As we will discuss in the last chapter, the Cryptocurrency market is highly manipulated. Often, the market makers trigger the stop-losses by breaking the patterns in the wrong direction so that it can liquidate the positions before it continues moving oppositely. These are the downsides of setting stop-losses in Cryptocurrency markets but being cut short on a small loss is still more rational than being exposed to the complete downfall.

Position sizing

The amount of money you are putting into a specific coin should highly depend on the risk associated with it. You should not put the same amount into a micro-cap as you would into a top 10 coin. The golden rule says, "never risk more than 1-2% per trade" but as easy as it might sound, it often gets misinterpreted.

Risking 1-2% does not mean that this is how much of your overall portfolio you are allowed to invest in a single trade. It means that this is the amount you can lose on that trade, which is an entirely different thing. Let us show you how this is different, by presenting @CryptoRedPill's example:

(Let's say our trading stack = 100k. 2% risk of that is $2000. We enter a trade with a stop loss 8% below my entry. So, 8% of how much is $2000? $25,000. So, you would be actually using 25% of your stack but only risking 2%.)

As you can see, the 1-2% does not represent the amount invested but the amount being at risk. On low caps where you usually do not have stop-losses, the invested money would not exceed that 1-2%, because there is no way of minimising the risk. On the higher caps, however, that is not the case.

Cutting losses

This is probably our favourite rule – cut your losses short & let your winners run. Never be afraid of selling your bag for a loss if you feel that the losses might get a lot bigger (based on TA, end of the market cycle, FUD incoming). People often tend to say HODL whenever they get underwater with their position. This speaks more about their inability to trade rather than this being a real strategy. There no single reason why anybody should be holding the coin through prolonged downtrend or incoming dip (selling the news). Not selling the coin and staying underwater until you break even is an opportunity cost – when the bag was frozen you could have made a few other profitable trades.

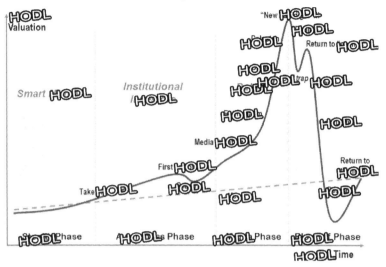

(The picture was taken from: http://swiatbitcoina.pl/poradniki/hodl/)

(Although this graphic is humoristic, it shows how actually a lot of people play market cycles. Do not mistake that with being an "investor". This simply shows that a person cannot adjust to the market conditions.)

During the opposite situation – when the coin is pumping – we suggest letting it run along with the trend. As we mentioned previously, taking profits on the way up is extremely important, but the nature of crypto makes it very hard to predict where the exact top is. Even if you are planning on exiting your position at a certain level, we always suggest leaving a so-called "moon bag". This is a small portion of the remaining position (for us it is 10%) that is left in case the coin decides to rise even further. This not only allows you not to FOMO back into it, as we already have the position, but it also often brings good profits.

(A good example is our trade on XRB in 2017. From 10 cents the price surged to 3 dollars which resulted in a very

respectable 30x return on the investment. We sold most of the position but left the previously mentioned "moon bag" of around 20% to catch the eventual blow-off top, although the coin already felt topped-out. To our surprise, this was not the end as XRB proceeded to reach 30$ during the following days. Even if we did not catch the other 10x with our whole position, we left a position significant enough to make a good return on that x300 at the top.)

Overtrading

This is probably what the new traders struggle with the most. When you see so many coins on the market pumping simultaneously, you feel an urge to catch every single one of them. In reality, unless you are good at trading quick swings, this attitude will cost you a lot of potential profits. The primary source of income comes from being patient and letting your early entry grow in value, not from constant buying and selling. Holding for a few days for 100/200% profits is much easier achievable than making several 10-15% swings to reach the same result. And yet, not many people decide to do that.

The quicker you realise you cannot catch every pump out there, the quicker you will start making money. Cutting your position before it can show its potential, and jumping into a new coin usually results in two things:

- Leaving a coin before it has a chance to pump

- Entering a coin, not at the bottom (decreasing profitability and increasing risk)

If not for potential profit, we highly suggest more patience and confidence in your investment because of a smaller chance of buying in on a bad entry. Never, no matter how strong the project is, enter the position on a big green candle. As we have mentioned before, it is better to entirely miss the pump than be at immediate risk of falling underwater.

Besides that, not overtrading gives you more time to do other things, and it does not cause emotional fatigue.

Falling for shills

If this was not clear enough already, every decision that you do should be yours and yours only. You can look to the other traders for a different perspective and new ideas, but other people should never be a deciding factor in taking a trade. By going though crypto-related social media channels, you will meet a lot of people promoting their bags. This should quickly teach you how to resist (more on this topic in the last chapter). Nobody takes responsibility for your lousy trade besides you; therefore, it is essential that you always rely only on yourself when making an investment decision.

Accumulating/taking profits

We talked about this already so this is only a small reminder – be patient with your entries and do not be afraid to take profits. Worst case scenario, you are going to miss some gains, best case you will get an excellent entry and additional money to play other opportunities.

Arbitrage

Arbitrage is just another opportunity on the market that, compared to regular trading, is associated with much smaller risk and more precise potential gains. It means taking advantage of the price differences between the exchanges – buy low on one and sell higher on another. The problem is that it works mostly on the markets with high liquidity and Cryptocurrencies are far from that.

Trying to profit from arbitrage opportunities in the Cryptocurrency market is tricky. We would not recommend it simply because actual trading offers much better ROI and often those opportunities disappear as quickly as they appear. Due to the often-long transfer time of coins between the exchanges, the price difference usually plummets before you manage to take advantage of it. Even if you manage to transfer the coins on time, very often the price difference would be the result of low liquidity on one of the exchanges. This means that to buy or sell your coins you would have to move the price which decreases your potential gains. Of course, by setting bids or sells orders you could hope for getting them filled – but as the rest of the market operates on prices different from that exchange, you could only hope that somebody makes the mistake of differing from the current value. Playing simple price swings in most cases would probably be more profitable anyway, as most arbitrage opportunities rarely go beyond 10%, which even for an inexperienced trader, is nothing.

The best arbitrage opportunities seem to exist between multinational exchanges. Very often prices of individual coins in Asia differ from European prices, but it is not easy to be registered in both markets. Since we never tried anything like this, we would instead focus more on trading itself, as that is where the real opportunities await.

Margin Trading

The first and most important thing about margin trading – playing with leverage is extremely risky and requires a lot of experience. It is not recommended for people just starting with trading, especially if they have no TA background. It is very tempting as it allows a trader to grab profits exceeding the portfolio, but very few people are successful with it.

While trading with leverage, you can either long or short your position. You buy a certain amount of contracts (where one contract equals one dollar) and depending on what option you took, you increase or decrease in value. Taking a long position is the same as you would try to swing a regular trade – you buy as low as possible and sell as high as possible. Shorting means the opposite – you are trying to catch the top, and you exit your position once you feel the price might start moving up again.

The leverage aspect that lures everybody into margin trading brings a lot more opportunities to the table. Depending on the platform, it is even possible to use 200x leverage, which is no different than gambling (basically anything above 25x should be considered more of a lottery than trading unless you are experienced). Trading this way allows you to enter the trade with a larger amount of cash than you possess. An example:

(Let's say you own 1000$. You would like to open a long position with all of it, so it means you are buying 1000 contracts at the specific price of your entry. If you would like to play with leverage, it would be possible for you to buy a bigger number of contracts. Leverage 5x would allow you to trade with 5000 contracts and 100x as if you had 100000$ on your account (even though you still have only 1000$ in real life). Whatever you win is counted by the number of contracts bought so 10% without leverage you would win 100$ and 10% on 100x leverage you would win 10000$.)

This is why margin trading is so popular and at the same time addicting. This opportunity, however, does not come for free, as it is much easier to get liquidated on leverage which equals losing your whole position.

Liquidation is the level at which the platform is taking away your whole position from the trade (you lose everything you put into the trade). If you are going long, that level is below your entry, and if you are going short, that level is above it. The leverage aspect here makes the liquidation level a lot closer to your entry making it easier to lose your money.

(Entering a trade with high leverage also proportionally increases your losses. A 10% fall of the coin on a trade without leverage would cost you 100$ (if you entered with 1000$). However, if you entered the same trade with 10x leverage, that same 10% would mean you already got liquidated because it equals 100% of your initial stack.)

Trading with high leverage is risky also for people who do not have much experience. It is too risky because the market is often manipulated and there are times when the price action is steered in a way that would trigger one of the sides (either longs or shorts).

(This is a 5-minute candle that covered a 750$ area on a Bitcoin move, at the same time liquidating a lot of high leveraged positions. This is not a rare view as this kind of moves happen very often especially during consolidation phases.)

The same methods that we would apply in regular trading apply here as well – stop-losses, appropriate position sizing, taking profits. We would not recommend trading with leverage higher than 5x unless you are experienced and are incredibly proficient in TA. Otherwise, this does not differ from gambling, and it is a wasted opportunity as the market is full of other options to profit from.

We highly recommend going through some Bitmex tutorial videos on YouTube and being very careful once you start trading with leverage – from experience we can confirm it is incredibly addictive and makes it almost impossible to leave the charts. If you ever find yourself thinking about your opened position, while you are not actively trading, it means you should neither play with such risks nor that your trade management is good enough if you have reasons to worry.

These topics that we just covered should be enough for you to put this book away and start taking your first steps in the cryptosphere world. However, as repetition is the mother of learning and as a small cheat sheet, we prepared a list of trading tips of what we talked about up to this point. These are the essentials thanks to which our fellow traders and we were successful in this field.

Trading tips:

- Never invest more than you can lose. That seems obvious but the majority of people we talked to during the bear market were overexposed not only in altcoins but with their wealth as well.

- Be humble—do not think you are the God of trading just because you caught a good pump. Everybody can catch a 10x during an alt season. Never stop learning and understand that it is the profit's sustaining that is hard—not making it.

- Fundamentals show you what you should buy, but it is the Technical Analysis that tells you where you should do it.

- To gain more experience you will have to go through significant losses as well. Only then will you appreciate the value of a well-thought strategy for minimizing risks. Do not give up even when you have a bad streak and stay true to your plan.

- Your goal is to always outperform the market. If you are holding a coin that increases in USD value but decreases in BTC, it means you are losing. You would be more profitable by simply holding Bitcoin, therefore always adjust your strategy in a way that would allow you to gain more than the market itself.

- Majority is usually wrong. Try counter trading the public opinion – when everybody thinks a coin will moon it probably will not. The markets are profitable because for every winning trade there is a losing one as well. To be on the former side you need to outperform most traders, not join them.

- Always look at the big picture. If you are investing do not be discouraged by a small pullback – zoom out and be patient. Best gains are never done by chasing coins, it is the waiting that is rewarded most.

- Never fall in love with your investment. You are here first and foremost to make profit, trade according to charts and fundamentals, your sympathy for the project comes second.

- Do not be afraid to take profits. The potential of catching another Verge-like pump is very tempting, but chances of that happening are extremely small. Instead of looking for one 100x, try combining few trades to reach the same target (4x,5x,5x gives you the same result and is a lot easier to achieve).

- Listen to other people's ideas but do not follow them. If you find yourself having a hard time taking a trade without somebody else's confirmation, it means you are not ready to trade yet.

- If you ever find yourself very emotional while trading, it means that your risk management is lacking. We suggest trading on paper first (without real money) to get used to decision process.

- Understand the feelings that rule the market. Do not let them affect you whether it is fear at the bottom or excitement at the top. Having a trading diary will help you to control your emotions.

- Entry is more important than the pump itself. It is better to miss a pump than enter in a wrong spot and instantly be underwater with your position.

Cryptosphere

In this chapter we would like to present a wealth of information about the Cryptocurrency market which did not fit with previous parts of the book. Since the technology is still new, the community around it is also small and can be very beneficial if used correctly. We will talk about useful tools for trading, describe the best of exchanges and talk about how not to let Cryptocurrencies take over your personal life.

Trusting crypto community

Some people call Cryptocurrencies the best distribution of wealth there has ever been, and it is hard not to agree when we see all those 20-year olds changing their lives thanks to this market. Since we live in times where social media has become the primary means of communication between young people, Cryptocurrencies are no different as new generations dominate them. Leading social media platforms include Facebook, Reddit and most importantly, Twitter. That is, apart from private groups being active on Telegram and Discord where the access usually must be requested.

Having an account on those channels is essential to doing proper research – it provides you with a community to share ideas with, a lot of rumours and news that you would not find anywhere else and a vast base of knowledge from the best traders out there. Since Twitter possesses the most significant number of experienced traders (from our experience of using Facebook and Reddit as well), we would highly suggest having an account on one of these platforms to soak everything cryptosphere has to offer. It is not only an excellent research base but also a fun place where you will be able to network with the most creative and exciting personalities this market can offer.

The growing popularity of Cryptocurrencies on social channels has also lead to the appearance of influencers that in such a small community can have enormous powers. We can confirm that from our experience as one of us also owns an account of significant size as well. Most of the big accounts are 100% anonymous, hiding behind cartoon avatars without revealing real data about themselves. It is probably the only place on the whole internet where multi-millionaires hidden behind a picture of a whale get into daily interactions with the world's famous entrepreneurs, celebrities or even pornstars. As a result, that popularity leads to them being able to influence the market in various ways.

(Having a big account (which starts from about 20 thousand followers on Twitter) gives you the ability to move in smaller markets. We personally (with 19000 followers) were experiencing instant pumps (10-20%) on the coins that we posted online, even if that wasn't our intention. There are profiles out there with about 50/100/150 thousand followers that continuously cause small pumps whenever a coin is mentioned, even on the high liquidity exchanges like Binance.)

It is a natural occurrence that a lot of people are trying to build a brand of their own because that gives a lot of benefits to the person. Having followers not only helps in research (as people interact with you and often share their results with you) but also provides a lot of opportunities to earn money, which is probably the most significant threat we would like to warn you about.

Being a big personality on Twitter not only allows you to cause movements on the market but also attracts companies offering money to promote their products (usually ICOs but other coins do this as well). Since money makes the world go round, a lot of people are taking this opportunity to earn extra profits, without disclosing their real intentions. Unfortunately, this happens all too often; therefore, you should always do your own research and keep this in mind.

Twitter has a culture of shilling coins to later brag about the gains if the made call brought good results. This is often done to increase the hype and pump their investment. Twitter and other social channels are a great way of getting information, but number one rule should be never to trust anything or anyone you see in there. If you ever find yourself having a hard time making an investment decision without confirmation from another trader, it means you are just not ready to trade yet.

(We know many traders that do paid promotions themselves and the consequences for people falling for those shills are often hard to watch. Only recently, at the end of a 3-month-long downtrend (March 2018) you could have seen dozens or hundreds of people attacking traders that lured them into ICOs that ended up being 80% below initial prices when listed. It is their fault that they fell for the shill, but it should also be a lesson for anyone else to watch out who you look up to.)

Let's continue and take a look at the name of this subchapter more precisely – who is trustworthy in the crypto community? Let's not put everybody into one basket and let's see how you can benefit from being a part of the community:

- Learn from the charts – as we mentioned in the TA chapter, there is no right or wrong way to create charts as everybody has their own style that either works for them or not. Being exposed to dozens of traders every one of which has a different approach to TA helps enormously to grow as a chartist. Study which indicators bring the most success and compare those scenarios with your trading ideas – this way, you will always have many different perspectives on how trade can play out.

- Look for unknown tickers – go through random threads and look for people shilling their coins. You would be surprised how often the biggest gainers appear in threads like this before a big profile picks them up and the run starts. Never fall for the suggestion of investing but always do your own research on it as once in a while that shill might be a potential big mover that nobody talks about yet.

- Form a group – there is only so much a single person can do, whether it is research or charting through the whole exchange. With so many good traders in the cryptosphere, there is no reason why you should not reach out to other people to share ideas and help each other. It not only takes a lot of weight – in this case, work- from your shoulders but also opens you up to the parts of trading you might not be good at (finding very low caps, margin trading – you name it).

- Be up to date with all important events – if you can filter through some apparent shills, you will be able to understand what is currently going on in the market and maybe find some excellent investment opportunities along the way. Have all the important events that are promoted on your radar, as there is perhaps something happening with your coin as well that you were not aware of.

One last thing that we would like to address in this topic is paid groups. It is a common phenomenon that during the bull market there are a lot of traders (appearing out of nowhere) that open paid signal groups – a place where you pay a monthly fee, where your "guru" gives you buy/sell signals that theoretically should outperform the market. We understand that there is a massive demand for that kind of service because not everybody has enough time to learn about trading themselves or spend so much time in front of the computer. However, as we have experienced two of the most massive alt seasons ever, we can confidently say that the vast majority of these groups are not worth the money. During a serious bull run losing money is almost impossible, as even blind guesses tend to give 50-100% gains (this is not an exaggeration, the crypto market is very irrational in its growth during alt season).

(We have been part of some of these groups ourselves to see how they work from the inside. Successful traders often

outperform the market with their calls, and we will not take that away from them. Things, however, get interesting when the bull market takes a break, and people must be guided through retracements. We have seen groups holding through 70% losses as the group owners were not able to give profitable calls during the bear market. That is apart from the fact that besides the calls, the majority of those groups never tried to teach the members a thing about trading and solely focused on giving signals to follow.)

We could count groups worth joining on the fingers of one hand, at least from the traders that are present on Twitter (we will not comment on other platforms as we are not aware of how the groups work there). If you need a service like this, because you lack time, make sure you talk to the current members. Get honest confirmation that the group makes profits in both, bull and bear markets and that it provides lessons on how to trade as well. Otherwise, we highly recommend learning how to trade by yourself. Not only because it will save you money from the fees, but because there is much free content to learn from by yourself (more on that later in this chapter). Knowing how to trade will not only bring you a quick profit now but will also remain a valuable skill for the future as you can use your knowledge for stocks as well. Trading requires enormous amounts of self-control and patience that cannot be achieved by following calls from others, as it comes strictly from experience and being on your own with a trade.

Market manipulation

Since the Cryptocurrency market has in most cases very low liquidity compared to regular markets, it is very prone to manipulation. This became an excuse for a lot of traders, as when the set-up they create does not work out they often tend to blame that on whales manipulating the price (which of course more often than not is just them being wrong). There is, however, no denying that the real whales often do have control over the specific market, so it is essential to know how to avoid being on the wrong side of the trade.

(Funny enough, while writing this chapter cryptosphere revealed one of the biggest dramas it has seen in a long time with a group of famous traders supposedly trying to control one of the markets (Haven, HXV to be more precise, a small coin with around 1 million market cap). The plan was to buy approximately 20 to 25% percent of the overall supply OTC (Over-The-Counter, outside of exchanges) to manipulate the price while trying to list it on more significant platforms to later dump their stack of coins after seeing massive gains. The plan was unsuccessful as they could not get organised and their ideas were revealed to the public by one of the traders, but it shows how even respected personalities can try to influence the market behind the doors.)

There is also a never-ending discussion on how much Bitcoin itself is manipulated (recently also with Cartel conspiracy theory), but since we have no specific answer to this, we will focus solely on altcoins and how bigger market players are controlling them.

Pattern fake-outs

As we mentioned in the TA chapter, Cryptocurrencies tend to follow price movements very precisely; therefore, it is easy for market makers to trigger stop-losses and trap breakout traders. As many traders put their SL just below the important support, the price is often manipulated so that it fakes a move down to trigger those orders and then moves into the other direction, with a substantial volume. Same goes the other way – breakout traders play the patterns by buying the moment when price decides its course, so the market makers allow that to happen to dump the price a moment later leaving the buyers underwater.

It is relatively easy to avoid both of those situations – in the first case make sure not to have your SL right below the critical support but a bit underneath it. This way you will still protect yourself from a more significant crash, but in case of a fake-out, your order will not get triggered. As for the false breakouts – if you are planning to buy them, make sure that the buying volume drastically jumped along with the candle. If the volume is low, wait it out a bit as it is better to miss out on a move than enter on a local top.

Price suppression

This is, in general, a positive thing for the price, as most of the time, it means the whales are accumulating coins. Price suppression can be evident on the chart itself, but most of the time we would use an order book to analyse it.

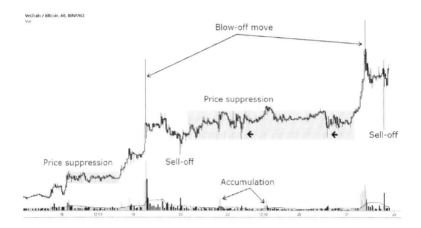

A high buy/sell walls on the order book are a way for the more prominent players not to buy or sell their positions but to change the way the market moves. If you are seeing them, it should give you either a signal to enter or exit depending on what the action looks like. In general, it goes like this:

- Sell wall – market maker is setting big wall on a sell-side to scare the potential buyers so that they can scrap lower bids and accumulate the position. People think that there is no chance for "eating" that wall, making them sell their position before it goes even lower.

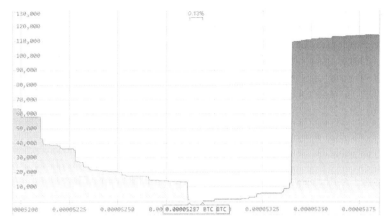

- Buy wall – market maker is setting big wall on a buy side to give the buyers more confidence so that they can exit their position on higher bids when people feel comfortable with the support below them.

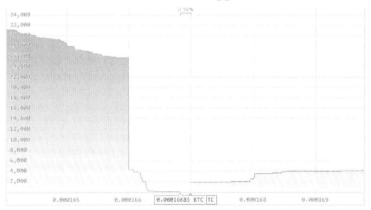

If you want to get excited about having real buy support behind you, make sure that the bids are spread evenly and on logical levels (near the support). Otherwise, trusting one big bid order might result in you getting underwater with your position. Same goes the other way – seeing one big wall should be a positive sign for you, as the market makers have interest in that specific coin. Unless there is a significant disparity between buy and sell side, do not pay too much attention to it, as those are simple games to shake out smaller players.

News manipulation

If you ever participated in both bull and a bear markets, you probably saw how much more active the development teams are when it comes to updates on their coins during uptrends and how quiet they are during downtrends. It is not a coincidence that the best news comes out during high times especially for lower caps, as the teams try to benefit as much as possible from the positive sentiment and price increases. The real manipulation, however, usually comes not from the team itself but the people interested in the coin.

As we are dealing with a low liquidity market, sometimes a single tweet can move a specific market up or down if its power is significant enough. Regarding the news, we will be dealing with either a rumour (per "buy the rumour sell the news" rule) or the FUD (per "It's simple FUD, don't listen to it"often heard from crypto traders). It is hard to speculate on the origin of most of these rumours that are circulating the community, but whether it is an organised action by whales or a random person trying to pump up the price, the results are often very similar.

(Very recently Dragonchain DRGN (260 million market cap at that time) was on the public radar as there was a rumour circulating about it being soon added to Bittrex, one of the most significant exchanges in crypto. Its source was a single tweet from an unknown account that quickly got picked up by all the more prominent personalities on Twitter, which made the price jump over 15% (not much but still). As it later turned out, the rumour was fake, and the listing did not happen as planned.)

(A previously mentioned Nucleus Vision NCASH was also an excellent example of one person having a significant influence on the price. It started with one Twitter profile sharing their conversation with big clothing brands that denied having anything in common with nCash which quickly begun circulating the whole cryptosphere. The price took a massive dip even though the supposed screenshots never got approved as legit and probably were faked before

other people started confirming the deals on their own. It does not matter if the partnerships were real or not in the first place – that one single screenshot was enough to affect the price of a coin with over 150 million in market cap.)

As you can see, even a tiny profile or screenshot can have an effect that goes into million gained or lost in the overall market cap of a coin. As it is tough to confirm who often stands behind those rumours, whether this is a planned operation or a random accident, it shows us one thing – manipulating the market based on falschoods is extremely easy and could be conducted quickly, if necessary. There is no real defence from it outside of proper risk management that we covered in the previous chapter, as that is the nature of emerging markets. What you can learn from this is that not everything you see has a real substance behind it – it is always worth verifying news you are reading so that you know if it is worth buying the dip or if it is time to cut the losses and move on to another position.

Impact on life

The impact crypto has on personal lives is a surprisingly rare topic among traders, even if many of them complain about the time they spend on crypto during the week. Since Cryptocurrencies never sleep (as the market works 24/7), there is always something happening, and opportunities never stop showing up.

Having an objective mind as a trader is pretty much correlated with having a healthy lifestyle. As much as we like the jokes circulating Twitter about Cryptocurrency traders never leaving their basements, it is not far from reality, as many traders indeed have terrible habits. There is a high chance that if you are already a trader, you had your share of trading days where you started your breakfast at 2 PM after a healthy amount of chart-watching in the morning.

As we have also experienced how Cryptocurrencies can take a toll on you when you do not set yourself some clear boundaries, these would be the tips we would suggest for every new member of this market:

- Do not spend too much time in front of the computer - do your research daily and check charts, but taking longer breaks will allow you to have a new perspective every time you come back to them.

- Have a regular day cycle – even if the crypto market works 24/7 it doesn't mean that you have to as well. Don't let the constant action get you and take advantage of the fact that you can plan your day however you want because of that continuous market availability.

- Take care of your body – exercise, eat healthily and sleep a lot. Physical shape is critical when it comes to trading as spending long hours in front of the chart takes a toll on your body, and mind as well as a result.

- Take care of your mind – try meditating and relaxing (in whatever form you prefer, whether these are books and for example games). Playing with significant amounts of money can create a lot of stress, which during extended periods can hinder your decision-making ability. Keep your emotions intact as otherwise, you will find yourself making rushed moves that you might regret later after the trade sorts out.

- Try separating trading from your private time – since the market is very exciting for all the people engaged in it, it is often hard not to mention it outside of your trading hours. You do not want to introduce your close environment to it, as often during the times when you want to take a break from trading, your circle of friends might remind you of it. No job should ever influence the personal life.

You may think this is pretty obvious and trivial, but if you have never traded in this market before you do not realise yet how addicting it becomes in a very short period. Making a lot of money often blinds a rational mind which might lead to bad decisions in the form of overtrading or losing perspective when is the right time to take profits. A sound strategy minimises the effect of emotions during trading as we explained that in the previous chapter, but not everybody has one from the beginning. For this reason, a responsible trader should always make sure that every decision he makes has a well-thought motive behind it.

Exchanges

The following description of exchanges will present the current (April 2018) state of them, so be aware that due to the dynamic nature of the market, this subchapter might not be as relevant in a few months from now. Apart from this, we would still like to give a fair overview of all the major exchanges on the market and what an investor can expect from them. A small note before we begin: the following list only presents the exchanges that in our opinion are worth using, mostly for trading altcoins. There are dozens of others besides those submitted by us, but if they were not listed, there must have been a reason for that (possibly due to low quality and no significant differentiation among the competition). Also, we recommend to chart on outside services (more on that later), because exchanges tend to have limited possibilities when it comes to conducting TA.

Before we conclude to show you, which Exchanges are worth using, we want to explain the nature of reference links. Reflinks are a way of inviting others to the platform (person A which is registered on an exchange asks Person B, and Person B can register with that link. It does not influence Person B, while Person A gets a bonus from the exchange). On many exchanges, such as Coinbase or Bitmex, a person invited is also rewarded with lowered fees. If you would like to support us and our work, we include our Reflinks under certain exchanges. Thank you in advance and let's continue with the chapter.

Big exchanges

Binance – currently (April 2018) the most popular exchange with the number one volume. It has seen a rapid rise to the top through less than a year and currently is the most used exchange among altcoin traders. Binance offers a relatively good variety of coins, and because of strict listing standards (and a high fee) usually, the projects are trustworthy (as much as that can be said about any crypto-related company. Very recently Binance was accused of buying coins before they get listed to profit from them. This happened with a currency called Bytecoin). The coins listed mostly consist of recently released ICOs with a small addition of already established projects from previous years. Excellent management that reacts to every potential attack/threat on the exchange. Overall a solid exchange, although should be approached with caution like any other centralised Cryptocurrency exchange.

REF: (Ref-ID: 29303036,
https://www.binance.com/?ref=29303036)

Bittrex – ex-biggest exchange before Binance took over. Lost its position and a lot of reputation because of frequent coin delisting (with no explanation provided) and closed registrations for a prolonged period. Currently, it is working again with new UI in place which has mixed reviews around the community. Since Bittrex is US-based, it is closely connected to SEC; therefore, the listing standards are one of the strictest in all crypto. It is a stable exchange with high volume, but we are not big fans of it because of the low variety of coins listed. Most projects on Bittrex are well-established coins that lack the interest new currencies are generating. It is a great place to practice TA as most coins have rich price history, but from the FA point of view – the more significant potential lies in other exchanges.

Honourable mention – Poloniex was the most popular altcoin exchange before Bittrex took the spot. In the middle of serious development currently, so not worth mentioning yet, but we suggest following the work being done as Circle acquired it.

Medium exchanges

KuCoin – KuCoin was named a "graveyard" during the recent downtrend (January-March 2018) because every coin that was listed in there crashed and the whole exchange was deprived of volume. It is a reasonably new exchange that is usually the first bigger platform that all the better ICOs are getting listed on. The fundamentals of the coins listed are solid and provide good risk/reward ratio as many of them will proceed to get listed on more meaningful exchanges, giving now a good chance for early entry.

REF: (Ref-ID: HKe8yy,
https://www.kucoin.com/#/?r=HKe8yy)

Bibox – KuCoin's twin brother for Chinese coins. A reasonably new exchange as well, with a smooth UI that is still hovering under the radar of many because the projects listed there usually are not known to the public eye yet. Majority of coins on Bibox come from China and provide an exciting alternative to popular ICOs, as fundamentally they present similar potential but are lacking exposure on more global markets. An excellent place to research coins that wouldn't land on your regular exchanges.

REF: (Ref-ID: 11361981,
https://www.bibox.com/signPage?id=11361981&lang=en)

Huobi – a good mixture between KuCoin and Bibox as it lists both new ICOs and a lot of Chinese coins as well. With a solid UI and constant development, it might not stand out with anything significant, but it's a good exchange to research "gems", as new listings are frequent and the platform has top 5 volume (April 2018).

REF: (Ref-ID: 5pwb3, https://www.huobi.br.com/de-de/topic/invited/?invite_code=5pwb3)

Small exchanges

Cryptopia – a smaller exchange that is famous for owning a vast amount of so-called "shitcoins". Cryptopia is a heaven for people looking for cheap masternode coins and some potential "gems", but overall the majority of coins in there have little to zero value. This exchange is often used for pump & dump strategies as the liquidity is non-existent in most trading pairs, therefore, seeing 300/400% daily pumps are not a rare view on Cryptopia. It is possible to find valuable projects if one manages to filter all the bad coins, so we would suggest using it for occasional high risk/high rewards plays. We also advise caution as there were recent reports of Cryptopia not processing withdrawals.

REF: https://www.cryptopia.co.nz/Register?referrer=Traderhand book

CoinExchange – another exchange with a bunch of very risky, low liquidity coins that in most cases have no value. Usually, we would not recommend using it, but during bull markets when people are looking for other opportunities after initial pumps, they often end up going for low caps which CoinExchange is full off. Not a place for regular trading but with extensive research using it might be rewarding as these coins have the potential to give a 10x type of gains in a matter of days.

Decentralized exchanges

IDEX – IDEX is the Ethereum decentralised exchange where the user has control over his private keys. Besides this small difference, the trading itself is basically the same as with other exchanges, as the UI is surprisingly good (we had a bad experience in the past with EtherDelta, to mention an example). The main advantage of decentralised exchanges is the speed at which new coins are being listed, and IDEX is a real gold mine when it comes to tokens. Mostly those are the newest ICOs that just finished their crowd sale, but older ETH-related projects are also being regularly listed. Since it is an Ethereum exchange the only projects that are being listed are the ones also working on the Ethereum Network. NEO also has one, and it is called Switcheo.Network which is also a decentralised exchange but for NEP-5 tokens (NEO Network).

Cryptobridge – Cryptobridge is another decentralised exchange that has been very popular in the last months because of their staking program (owning BCO coins and staking them, gives you a part of the overall fees from the exchange). It is not as intuitive as IDEX in its use but owns a share of quality PoW projects that are worth opening an account in there. It still lacks any significant volume, but since DEXes are only starting to get more recognition, this should not last long until it has more liquidity.

Others

Coinbase – the number one platform when it comes to buying/selling Bitcoin, which also features a few other main Cryptocurrencies like Ethereum or Litecoin. It is indeed not a platform for trading itself (no charts, only 1-click buys/sells) and fees are relatively high, but it is worth monitoring as it is currently the main gateway for people wanting to get into crypto. Any coin listed there would probably experience an enormous increase in value and recently added support for ERC20 tokens sparks a lot of rumours daily.

GDAX – basically like Coinbase, but a bit more professional. Here you have an advanced optic and significantly lower fees (you need to create a limit order and pay 0,25% (April 2018) instead of 1,49% on Coinbase). Many people do not know about this as it is not as convenient as the Coinbase's main page. To work with GDAX, you need to put FIAT money in your Coinbase account and then transfer the FIAT money within the Coinbase website to GDAX. Then you can register with your Coinbase access.

REF: https://www.coinbase.com/join/594390c5a5ee7507808399 12

Bitmex – a number one platform for margin trading (up to even 100x). Extremely popular among traders because of reflinks that provide additional profits from every person that signs up from their recommendation. As we mentioned in the previous chapters, we do not recommend playing with leverage unless you are experienced with technical analysis. Do not fall for prominent twitter personalities encouraging to start margin trading, as usually only one side of this deal comes out profitable.

REF: https://www.bitmex.com/register/SMlFsf

Bitfinex – one of the most significant exchanges that enable margin trading as well. It is also the only exchange with a more extensive variety of alts that have their trading pairs with USD. Currently (April 2018) many legal issues are surrounding Tether and Bitfinex concerning audit and money laundering.

Important tools

Coinigy / TradingView – a must-have tool for every Cryptocurrency trader. It is a charting site that offers you precision and tools not available on any exchange. We prefer TradingView because of the UI that is more appealing but Coinigy is not far off, and it offers more compatible exchanges. Main differences present like this:

- TradingView – slightly better UI, free to use up to 3 indicators, a big community of traders to share ideas with, only most significant exchanges

- Coinigy – free for the first 30 days, the same set of tools as TradingView but allows charting smaller exchanges as well (even low liquidity ones like Cryptopia)

Blockfolio/Delta – an application that helps you track your portfolio. It is essential not only to check your current balance but also to put on alarms on specific price points (for example when an exchange does not have a stop-loss option, alerts are essential to minimise potential losses). Just don't get addicted to checking it every 5 minutes- we have all been there.

https://CoinMarketCap.com/ – a starting page for any Cryptocurrency trader. A database for every existing project out there (outside of tiny ones that are yet to be listed) additional info on overall market capitalisation, volume, biggest gainers and new additions. This is a place where you start your research.

https://coinmarketcal.com/ – a perfect tool not only for swing traders trying to catch some pumps based on news and events. This site lists all the upcoming developments for coins with a precise date and description to it. A useful website that can help you assess how your investment could perform in the forthcoming days/weeks.

https://bitcointalk.org/ – biggest Cryptocurrency forum out there that exists from the beginning. Currently, a bit abandoned as the majority of people moved to Twitter and other social media channels, but it is still an excellent tool for doing research. The best value is not in the coin-discussing threads (although there are useful tips hidden in there as well), but in the new [ANN]'s that are being posted for new coin listings. As we mentioned in the FA chapter – this is the earliest opportunity to catch a project that you can find in all crypto.

Social media – we suggest mostly using Twitter and occasionally Reddit, but no matter what you chose, social media channels should be your daily tool in trading. Beware of the dishonest promoting that we talked about earlier in this chapter, but there are too many benefits from following other traders not to take advantage of it. Build yourself a group of solid chartists and investors that you like as that will ease your own researching needs by a lot (for a list of people to follow – see the previous subchapter of sources of learning). Also, don't forget about the ticker searching method that we discussed in the FA chapter – it is the best way to understand the current sentiment around the coin.

ICOBench / ICODrops – sites that include all the ongoing and future ICOs. All the necessary information in one place – reviews, ICO metrics, White Papers. We always recommend whitelisting into even unknown ICOs (if the registration process is quick) because they tend to close very quickly and proper research can still be done later, without losing the opportunity of investing in a promising crowd sale.

https://coin360.io/ - gives you a broad overview of the whole market divided by different categories of your choice. This simple tool allows analysing which segment is currently on the rise or which one holds the price well when everything else dumps.

https://etherscan.io/ – a site that will enable you to check token's distribution and metrics such as circulating supply, in addition to Txns on Etherum Network. For coins on different blockchains use dedicated sites (for Bitcoin as an example - https://blockchain.info/).

https://airdrops.io/ - a place for all essential upcoming airdrops. Usually, they are not worth a lot, but by regularly participating in them there is a way to create a small source of constant income. You never know when the next Ontology might happen (an airdrop that was worth 9000$ after few weeks (April 2018)).

Sources of learning

Since the Cryptocurrency market is still a relatively new place, it is hard to find many good learning materials that would help new investors. As the cryptosphere grows, more people are willing to create valuable educational content, so below, we are presenting a small base to get yourself familiar with. As always, the best experience and knowledge will come from making your own mistakes during trading, but this book and the content presented will help you minimise the effects of them.

Sites

https://lopp.net/bitcoin.html

https://www.babypips.com/trading

https://www.investopedia.com/

https://medium.com/tag/Cryptocurrency

https://steemit.com/bitcoin/@joseph/wolong-the-game-of-deception-unedited-version

https://t.me/cryptorangutang

CoinMarketCap Alternatives

https://coinlib.io/

https://www.livecoinwatch.com/

https://www.coingecko.com/

https://coincheckup.com/

YouTube Channels

Crypto Cred

(https://www.youtube.com/channel/UCBaU9NXRPjkLGgJy-M7RPCw)

Josh Olszewicz

(https://www.youtube.com/user/carpenoctom)

Coin Bloq

(https://www.youtube.com/channel/UCrsEzLxi1oxHr6xW9S5vSzg)

The Cryptonomatron

(https://www.youtube.com/channel/UCXdsog7Jzmqo_AUX3zstSLg)

Ivan on Tech

(https://www.youtube.com/user/LiljeqvistIvan)

Julian Hosp

(https://www.youtube.com/user/julianhosp)

Twitter

Those are the people that we feel provide excellent value to the community. We encourage you to give them a follow but as always – do your own research. Keep in mind that these social media profiles are in no way meant to be professional and they present a very loose style of communication. We do not take responsibility for their future content.

Technical Analysis: @joezabb, @moolaland, @ledgerstatus, @cryptowilson, @CryptoCred, @CryptoTutor, @Beetcoin, @Anbessa100, @CarpeNoctom, @crypto_birb, @AngeloBTC, @crypToBanger, @anambroid, @ThisIsNuse, @overheardcoffee, @CaptainCoinigy, @CryptOrca, @koningkarell, @Broccolex, @cryptoWalk3r

Fundamental Analysis: @cryptorangutang, @growdigi, @notsofast, @needacoin, @bitcoin_dad, @Sicarious_, @bit_xan, @koreanjewcrypto, @CryptoMaestro, @Cryptomickey, @CryptoShillNye, @VerthagOG, @jiucrypto, @cointradernik, @cryptic_monk, @ubiqannbot

The End

Congratulations, you made it through the whole book and set the basis for a successful Crypto-Life. We want to thank you for your attention and interest into this complex topic. If you want to follow up on the newest analysis by Marcin Kacperczyk, you can follow "CryptOrangutang" on twitter (https://twitter.com/cryptorangutang). In the last chapter of this book, we will show you some interesting facts about Cryptocurrencies. We would be happy if you would recommend this book to your friends, helping us teach the rest of the world about Cryptocurrencies.

Before we conclude to the last section of this book, we want to take a moment to thank all the people that made this book happen.

We want to thank both, Fabian and Julian Möller, for publishing the book and providing support throughout the whole process.

Furthermore, we thank Nathalie Kratz for this fantastic cover. We are convinced you will become a great designer.

Special thanks to Thomas Zell and Haroula Konsta, for proofreading the English version.

Lastly, thanks to you for being interested in this topic and our work.

At the end of this book, we have gathered some interesting information about the Cryptoworld such as famous people, massive hacks and other fascinating facts. Have fun!

Famous People

Satoshi Nakamoto

One of the most significant secrets concerning Cryptocurrencies is the question who Satoshi Nakamoto is. We know he is the founder of Bitcoin and was active in several Bitcoin communities until 2010.

Since 2011, we haven't heard about him, and the conspiracy theories are growing. Many people assume he is of Japanese origin.

(In Japanese, Satoshi means clear thinking, Naka means within, or relationship and Moto means origin or inception. The problem is that each word can have more than one meaning)

Fact is, we cannot say who this person is, it could as well be a group of people. There are several assumptions based on language analysis which was used in Nakamoto's paper, but all of the assumed people denied being Nakamoto.

According to people who worked with him he was an extremely conscientious person.

You may question, how wealthy he is. Well, the answer cannot be given with absolute certainty, but it is estimated that Satoshi Nakamoto owns about 1 million Bitcoins, which would be about 8 billion USD (April 2018). There is no certainty if he ever is going to use it or if he is already dead. Everything concerning Satoshi is still pure speculation.

Vitalik Buterin

Probably the second most famous person in the Cryptoworld is Vitalik Buterin. The 24-year old (2018) Russian started programming at the age of 10, and at 19 he published the White Paper of his own Cryptocurrency Ethereum.

He got the idea by playing World of Warcraft (an online game, where players can buy items from one another), as he thought the payment system is way too complicated and started to work on an alternative.

Ethereum is the second largest Cryptocurrency with a vast potential and adaption possibilities.

John McAfee

One of the probably most polarising people in Cryptocurrencies is the 72-year old John McAfee. The founder of McAfee security is an IT specialist from Great Britain and one of the great minds in the programming world.

He is known for his eccentric personality and was addicted to drugs for a long time. Since the mid 80's, he is, by his own account, sober. He was responsible for the extreme hype of Verge (2000%) and is known for "shilling" coins, which continually leads to a lot of pump&dump accusations.

Roger Ver ("Bitcoin Jesus")

Roger Ver, another polarising personality, is the main person behind Bitcoin Cash and he gained most recent attention for insulting a YouTuber who called Bitcoin Cash "BCash". He claims that "Bitcoin Cash" is the real Bitcoin and believes that Cryptocurrencies are the most important invention since the internet.

He gave up his citizenship of the USA and lives in Japan since then. If you want to see the infamous interview - check out https://www.youtube.com/watch?v=oCOjCEth6xI

Largest Hacks

Mt. Gox

Mt. Gox was one of the largest exchanges in the world and was attacked by hackers twice. The exchange was founded by Jed McCaleb, the same person who founded Ripple.

The first time in June 2011 caused damage of 8,750,000 dollars and occurred because a hacker was able to access Mt. Gox auditor machine.

The second and more serious one took place in February 2014. The hack stole Bitcoins over the years and went by undetected by the security teams of Mt. Gox. (This is the reason why many people are sceptical if it was a hack or a false game to keep the funds for themselves). Around 750,000 Bitcoins of their customers were lost and 100,000 of Mt. Gox.

Value back then: 473,000,000$

Value (April 2018): 6,800,000,000$

The DAO Hacker

The DAO hack was one of the most significant hacks that shattered the Cryptoworld. A DAO is a Decentralized Autonomous Organization, which is working with smart contracts. People who wanted to participate traded Ether to DAO and in return received DAO tokens.

On the 18th June 2016, members of the Ethereum community recognised funds of DAO were drained. 3.6 million Ethers disappeared in the first hours. The attack was based on an exploit found in the splitting function of the network (a process which allowed the user to get back his Ethereum, which they sent to DAO).

Based on this, the hacker was able to request his funds back multiple times with the same DAO token. Therefore, he was able to steal 3.6 million Ether.

Because of that hack, Ethereum initiated a hard fork, which created Ethereum Classic.

Value back then: 70,000,000

Value (April 2018): 1,800,000,000

Bitfinex

Another exchange was hacked in August 2016. Bitfinex, at that time one of the largest exchanges lost 119,756 Bitcoins.

Until now it is not clear how the hacker was able to manipulate the withdrawal system. It remains the second largest Bitcoin hack.

Value back then: 72,000,000

Value (April 2018): 958,048,000

Parity Wallet

In July 2017, a hacker managed to access funds from the Parity-multi-sig wallet. The hacker was able to remove the coins without an authorisation. In total, he stole 153,037 Ether.

Value back then: 30,000,000

Value (April 2018): 76,518,500

These are examples why you should always store your coins in a safe place and do not leave them on an exchange (only the small coins/funds). Do never use an online seed / private key creator.

16 Fascinating Facts

1) How much do exchanges earn by collecting fees?

Binance is earning the highest revenues (April 2018), with 3.5 million dollars per day! Followed by Upbit (3.4m), Huobi (2.3m), Bittrex (2.2m) and Bitfinex (805k). Binance actually managed to have higher profits than the Deutsche Bank in the first quarter of 2018. 200 million dollars were earned with only 200 employees.

2) How much money was raised by ICOs in 2017 and what was the largest one?

Over 3.5 billion dollars were raised from all the ICOs in 2017. The ICO which collected the largest amount of money was Filecoin with 257 million dollars.

3) Has there ever been a hack of a blockchain?

No, as we learned, it is impossible to hack a blockchain. The media simply confuses exchanges with Cryptocurrencies.

4) What hash-rate does a human have?

A human would have a hash-rate which is about 0.00003 h/s. In comparison, a single graphic can make up to 30 MH/s.

5) What does "crypto" mean?

Crypto is an old Greek word and means hidden or secret. Initially, the word was connected to the science of encryption.

6) Could a Cryptocurrency work as a national currency?

Yes, it could. In fact, Venezuela created the "Petro" and is the first country which created a Cryptocurrency. Because of the deflation character of Cryptocurrencies, it should help the country, which suffers under hyperinflation.

7) *How many people know about Cryptocurrencies?*

Studies found out that about 80% of the U.S. American students have never heard about Bitcoin, which is the most famous Cryptocurrency (End of 2017). Scientific projections assume there are about 50 million active Cryptocurrency traders and users (end of 2017). Some experts believe that this number will snowball to over 250 million within the next three years.

8) *How likely is it to guess a private key of another person?*

It is more likely to win the lottery five times in a row and then be hit by a bolt of lightning than to guess the private key of another person.

9) *How much money could banks save with the blockchain technology?*

Banks could save 8 billion dollars or more per year if they used the blockchain technology.

10) *How fast is the global crypto market growing?*

The global crypto market is the fastest growing market in the world. In 2015, the market rose from 5 billion to 7 billion (40%). In 2016, from 7 billion to 16 billion (128%). In 2017, from 16 billion to 570 billion (3500%). Experts claim the total market cap will increase to 20 trillion by 2024.

11) *What was the most massive Pump and Dump?*

It is hard to judge which of the Pump and Dumps were the largest ones, because of different duration, volume and percentage. There are so many coins that pump around 1000-2000% such as MAZA, AUR and ZETA. The latter is an excellent example of a regular pump and dump coin.

12) *What was the largest Scam in the history of Cryptocurrencies?*

The most massive Scam in history was BitConnect. The Ponzi scheme was one of most abundant in the financial history. From April 2017 to January the 9Th in 2018 the price increased from around 10$ to more than 440$, until the founders approved the fraud and got away. Within one day the price fell below 20$ and currently is at 0,94$ (Mid of January 2018).

13) *Who was the first Bitcoin billionaire?*

The Winklevoss twins were the first Bitcoin billionaires. You might know them because they claim Facebook was their idea that had been stolen by Mark Zuckerberg. The Winklevoss twins received 65 million dollars from Zuckerberg and invested 11 million of it in Bitcoin at a price of only 100$.

14) *Who owns the largest active wallet?*

The FBI seized a wallet by a black-market site containing over 144,000 BTC making the FBI the largest active wallet owner. There is one address containing more BTC, but it is unused for years. Many people think this is the wallet owned by Nakamoto. It is estimated that he mined around 1 million BTC.

15) *What was the most expensive pizza ever?*

Yes, you read correctly, on May 22nd in 2010 Laszlo Hanyecz paid 10,000BTC for two pizzas, which now would be worth over 80,000,000 $ (March 2018). It is known as the first item which was bought with Bitcoin. This day is also called Bitcoin Pizza Day.

16) *How dangerous are quantum computers?*

There is a high degree of danger, but not only for Cryptocurrencies. Quantum computers are extremely powerful, and they cannot be built yet. Experts are discordant when they are invented (20-40 years could be realistic). Many people claim quantum computers are the most significant fear of Bitcoin and Co., but this is not the case as a lot of Cryptocurrencies such as IOTA, QRL are resistant against this threat.

Bibliography

Murphy, John J. Study Guide for Technical Analysis of the Financial Markets: a Comprehensive Guide to Trading Methods and Applications. New York Institute of Finance, 1999.

Hosp, Julian. Crypto Currencies: Bitcoin, Ethereum, Blockchain , ICO's & Co. Simply Explained. Lightning Source, 2017.

https://twitter.com/CryptoRedPill/status/963288008341385217

https://twitter.com/CryptoCobain/status/922197320292323328

https://www.youtube.com/watch?v=cP_YwNhgh98

https://www.youtube.com/watch?v=HOIucvo-9s0&t

https://www.youtube.com/watch?v=J6pMoZM5zwA&t

https://www.youtube.com/watch?v=9464CKHbVA8&t

https://medium.com/@CarpeNoctom/toshimokus-trading-tips-tricks-f0ff5cc38cc8

https://cointelegraph.com/news/volumes-on-most-major-Cryptocurrency-exchanges-are-fake-or-inflated-study

https://steemit.com/deutsch/@achim86/heute-ist-blockchain-morgen-ist-hashgraph

https://www.blockchainmoney.de/assets/Was-ist-Hashgraph.pdf

https://www.bitcoinmining.com/what-is-proof-of-work/

https://en.bitcoin.it/wiki/Proof_of_work

https://www.computerwoche.de/a/blockchain-technologien-im-detail,3330877,2

https://www.nasdaq.com/article/what-is-the-tangle-and-is-it-blockchains-next-evolutionary-step-cm911074

https://coin-hero.de/power-ledger/

https://ark.io/

https://www.ccn.com/fundamental-principles-utility-tokens-blockchain-ecosystem/

https://strategiccoin.com/difference-utility-tokens-equity-tokens/

https://www.maxblue.de/robin/magazin_was-ist-ein-etf.html?utm_medium=referral&utm_source=taboola&cookieTest=check

https://medium.com/tokenreport/filecoin-v-sia-storj-maidsafe-the-crowded-push-for-decentralized-storage-7157eb5060c9

Printed in Great Britain
by Amazon

52443726R00170